Rugbaean

Transatlantic Rambles

Inktank publishing

Rugbaean

Transatlantic Rambles

Inktank publishing, 2018

www.inktank-publishing.com

ISBN/EAN: 9783747773536

TRANSATLANTIC

RAMBLES;

OR,

A Record of Twelve Months' Travel

IN THE

UNITED STATES, CUBA, & THE BRAZILS.

BY A RUGBÆAN.

LONDON: GEORGE BELL, 186, FLEET-STREET; AND
G. AND T. BROOKE, DONCASTER.
MDCCCLI.

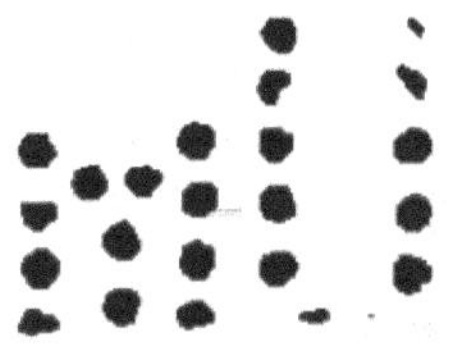

PREFACE.

A PREFACE—what about? If there is a species of publication that requires a preface less than another, it is a record of foreign rambles, or a rambling record, as some keen critical schoolfellow (a mere football-kicking being ten years ago) may very likely grumble out as he glances through the following pages. But as the author supposed that some "leaded" letter press between the title-page and the "departure from the white shores," &c. was absolutely necessary, he got into a long mixed train of thought about what form of preface that letter-type ought to embody;—whether it should be an affectionate preface, eulogising some relation, friend, or patron; whether a politico-philosophical preface, inculcating some great general principle which was to be illustrated and elucidated by the subsequent letter press; or whether an apologetico-explanatory preface, in which the author should endeavour to stave off from himself all the mistakes that the book contained.

After much consideration, he fixed upon a mild form of the latter, and having no friends who would care about marks of affection set forth in such a manner, not having heard of any one principle general enough to be illustrated by the following record, and not being fond of making apologies—he resolved that the preface should be bluntly expl natory, and merely to say,—

Firstly, that all the following nineteen chapters originally appeared between March, '50, and March, '51, in a country paper, some of whose readers expressed a wish to have them bound up, and thus put into a more tangible shape for reference than could be arrived at if they continued wildly scattered through columns upon columns of bye-gone journals.

Secondly, that until two-thirds of the letters had been composed, he was even ignorant of the wish of his friends to publish them, and hence as the *matériel* of the chapters had to be extracted from matter intended for the amusement and edification of those friends only, due allowance must be made for their mutilated and hashed-up shape as well as for the very barren account of the travel up the Mississippi, and also the presence of that unshapely appendix to a book, a copious batch of errata.

And now these preliminaries being settled, the writer begs the adventurous person who has taken his book in hand, if he fears not a sea voyage, and cares not for the previous nausea that the above prelude or shore-boat to the adventures may have created, to accompany him on board the steamer and prepare as he did for the worst.

London, March, 1851.

INDEX.

ERRATA.

PAGE.		LINE.	
3	..	9	for [illegible] read [illegible].
10	..	10	for *Rorus House* read *Revere House.*
41	..	33	for *Levy Island* read *Long Island.*
50	..	35	for *Phillimore* read *Fillmore.*
67	..	27 & 29	for *Alhabama* read *Alabama.*
70	..	30	for *Arkusan* read *Arkansas.*
78	..	24	for *Mort al Papa* read *Morte al Papa.*
78	..	26	for *Vive al Papa* read *Viva el Papa.*
95	..	34	for *Arbrothas* read *Abrolhos.*
96	..	5 & 34	for *Cape Trio* read *Cape Frio.*
103	..	13	for *Laryo de Paco* read *Largo do Paço.*
106	..	8	for *Ilha das Cobras* read *Ilha das Cobras.*
110	..	16	for *Tejuca Peak* read *Tejucu Peak.*
—	..	—	for *Coacovado* read *Corcovado.*
114	..	7	for *Pacaie* read *Pacau.*
119	..	33	for *Vasquez de Gama* read *Vasco de Gama.*
152	..	10	for *espinkas* read *espinhas.*
158	..	32	for *chiaro-scuro* read *chiaroscuro.*
163	..	17	for *Englishman* read *Englishmen.*
166	..	36	for *no Englishmen* read *we Englishmen.*
168	..	4	for *Pics* read *Pies.*

Transatlantic Rambles.

CHAPTER I.

"For leagues along the watery way."
"Through gulf and stream my course has been."
Norna's Song.

THE VOYAGE OUT—SEA SICKNESS—FLIRTATIONS.

OUR proper time for leaving the Mersey was half-past two on the afternoon of Saturday, but in consequence of the delay of the mails, which are always behind their time, we did not weigh anchor till nearly four, by which hour the last letter bag had been pitched in, the last cheer given, and we were fairly off. The first of a passenger's numerous anxieties on board, is to select his luggage out of the mass of packages which cover the deck, and have that portion of it which he may require during the voyage, taken down at once into his berth. This selection is a matter of the utmost importance, as you may fancy the situation of any one who had the wrong packages stowed away in the hold, and had to look to a box containing merely his books and papers, to furnish him with the means of washing, shaving, and dressing for ten long days. These obstacles having been triumphantly surmounted, I went again on deck, and learnt from enquiry and observation that in consequence of the state of the tide, the pilot would only allow us to go at half-speed. Any reflections arising therefrom were disturbed by the steward and his bell, announcing dinner, at which 135 persons (60 of them ladies) gradually got

B

seated. All of them were in the highest possible spirits, and evidently prepared, while opportunity and the state of stomachs permitted, to do great execution. I sat by my friend J——, opposite a line of faces from nearly every nation—American, German, French, Spanish, and English; some with beards dipping into their soup-plates, others like the writer, with very small pretensions to anything of the sort; some using their forks as a medium of communication between their plates and their mouths; some their knives, some their fingers, but all highly merry, polite, and hungry. I am unfortunately seated next to a deaf old lady, whose principal failing seems to be, that she considers it "her mission" to hand bread perpetually to everybody within arms-length of her. *I* pray mentally that sickness may have removed her by to-morrow from her sphere of usefulness. Evening has been gradually closing in, and on going on deck, I find it is nearly dark and that they are sending up rockets as signals to some of the numerous pilot boats, to come and take up our pilot, a jolly red-faced man, who had been trying very hard to look anxious, and signally failed. At length we see a blue light in the distance, then another, and presently a pilot-boat in full sail comes out of the mist. She sends a little boat, in gets the pilot, we see something black dancing on the waters between us and the cutter, but we go at full speed, setting sails fore and aft, and soon everything is lost in the gloom. By the pilot I send two letters which I forgot to post at Liverpool. I am afraid they will reach their destination in rather a dirty state, as the varied contents of a pilot's pocket would scarcely bear analyzing. I have just been down to inspect the capabilities of my berth, which is much more roomy than I expected, and about twice the size of my old study at Rugby. The passengers begin to yawn and retire. I fall asleep, and do not wake till half-past eleven, when I begin to find my way down stairs. The berth above mine is already tenanted, but I see nothing except a snoring sort of white pyramid; the light is put out by some unseen process, and I find myself in darkness doing something with my portmanteau, with a view to opening it. I try to expostulate with the steward, but to no purpose, and at length find my way to bed and to sleep.

By the time I and my companion (who is a respectable-looking Scotchman, and the father of two children in the next berth, to whom he is perpetually shouting) are dressed, the bell rings for breakfast, at which we sat in the same order as at dinner, but there are a few vacancies; the deaf old lady has departed. On reaching the deck I find it is a splendid morning, with the Salteze, an island off Waterford, and the Irish coast very plain in the distance. I never saw the tints on the sea so beautifully brought out, but am told that we shall see them better in the Atlantic. The Captain is pointing out places along the coast to the passengers. He is a little man with nothing particular in his appearance, save and excepting a remarkably soft benevolent eye, which I should think is the reason why he is such a favourite amongst the ladies. We are to have no church service to day. The captain, who generally reads prayers, is supposed to be too much occupied with the dangerous navigation of the channel to perform that duty. It is very difficult to think it is Sunday, the novelty of shipboard is so strange, and the routine of ship life and ship duty so much the same as on a week day. We sail very fast, with the wind in our favour, and by six o'clock are off Cape Clear, and fairly started on the Atlantic. A little talkative American, a true specimen of a Republican, has been holding forth to a numerous audience on slavery. He quite disapproves of it, and thinks it must be abolished by a national, not an individual effort. From certain reasons, his epithets are considerably stronger than his arguments. I have been introduced to young ——, the son of the tragedian, and to a Colonel ——, who has served through the Sikh campaign. Tea and supper are duly announced and finished, and as Pepys would have it, "so to bed."

Another splendid morning, and the sea as smooth as possible for the Atlantic. Dolphins enjoying themselves on all sides. A little Quaker and his wife make great efforts after breakfast to get the passengers to join in a game, called "Devil take the hindmost," which is made by a double circle and "one out," whose object is to touch the hindmost person of any couple, when the person touched becomes the one out. The fun arises out of evading the touches, by, when you happen to be third, running out to place yourself at the head of the other two. At first the people were shy of it, but it gradually took, and gave rise to shouts of laughter, once especially when, from the slippery state of the deck, the colonel, the Republican, and the tragedian rolled one over the other. Leave Quakers alone say I for getting up a little fun! Towards evening the wind got up, with a nasty cross sea, and there is a sort of moaning through the rigging, which bodes unpleasant things. I have had a great deal of conversation with the Republican, who is a very sensible man, though his habits are somewhat strange, such as going about the table at dinner, and selecting out of each dish whatever he may chance to take a fancy to, with other little table cloth failings. To night I met him by the capstan, in the middle of the vessel, whither passengers repair to smoke and sleep, and got out of him that he was a ——— man, who had been devoting the last ten years of his life to planning a new way of turning spindles in a mule. He left America with a few dollars and his new invention in his pocket, and is now returning with a handsome fortune. His boast on the subject, I give, somewhat in his own words. "*I left America as poor as Job's turkey, but now I'll set up a mill on the banks of my native river, and before I die, I'll make ——— whip the universe, there's no mistake about that.*" You must know that "Job's Turkey" is a favourite Yankee metaphor for "poverty."

Tuesday and Wednesday I join into one, as I cannot remember anything particular happening in either of them. Our forebodings of Monday were but too true. A sou-wester got up during the night, and I awoke early, very sick and uncomfortable. Then succeeded hours on hours of dreariness, heat, sickness, and eccentric thoughts and musings, in which all the events of the last month at home and abroad, came crowding on the brain, taking the strangest forms and conjuring up the most ridiculous fancies; the whole surmounted by an overpowering sense of langour and weight in the back of the head, which was painfully diffused through the whole of this chaos of ideas. Sometimes an enquiring steward appears and disappears at the door, and now and then, J——, whose stomach neither nor-wester nor sou-wester can affect in the slightest, obtrudes his imperturbable visage, but his kind enquiries are vaguely answered and he retires. One of the Scotchman's children begins to howl miserably, and keeps on some whining, pitiful request, but no nurse interferes, and the father, who lies above me, seems to have lost all the feelings of a father, for he answers only by his own guttural sufferings, which are often painfully distinct. At last, after some rousing efforts to get out of my berth and on my legs (but finding it perfectly impossible to keep the latter, owing to the disturbed motion of the ship), I sit down on the floor and shout out for the steward, who, when he comes, says it is "Thursday morning, and a heavy sea on." By the afternoon, I manage to get something on, too, and stagger up to the saloon, where I find about thirty melancholy faces, whom the acknowledged wit of the cabin (a funny man, who has crossed the Atlantic forty-three times, and is always pleasant on the subject) is trying hard to enliven, but his jokes fall flat—his auditors are too listless to attend, too melancholy to appreciate. From the saloon windows occasional glimpses are to be caught of dark masses of sea hurrying by and towering over the bulwarks. Presently there is a savoury smell of dinner, and my feelings begin to get the better of me. I descend to my berth, and subsequently eat two helpings of cold beef shin, and feel all the better for it. Great improvement in weather and appetite brings a good company up next day to breakfast, but all with such faces! No one is shaved, beards have been allowed to grow recklessly, hairs springing up everywhere; everybody ravenous; people with carving-knives suggest the idea of brigands. J—— appears; J——, as neat as when I first saw him in London—not a hair out of place, not a ruffle in his shirt or countenance, but J—— clean-shaved, calm and courteous as ever. The sea still continues rough, and deck promenaders run a risk of becoming more thoroughly acquainted with the Atlantic foam than they could wish.

Saturday also brings with it a visible improvement in attendance and spirits. Ladies, dressed in divers peculiar head-dresses, wrappers, and *visites*, begin to appear. Dinner boasts of nearly as good a muster as on the first day, and people begin to be conversational and scandalous. Some begin to ask "who that lady is" who is always lying on a sofa, with a gentleman always leaning over her and exchanging gentle whispers? Somebody says she is a Mrs. ——, but wonders where Mr. —— is. Somebody then hazards an assertion that he is in England, some laugh, and a great many sympathise with him. The pretty lady, too, opposite, has a husband in a cabin below, where he has been extended in the lowest depths of squeamishness for full six days. Well! she, too, has certainly been seen in the saloon, or on the deck, talking and laughing with a fine-looking dark-eyed countryman (by whom she is sitting at present)—a senator in —— —far oftener and longer than with her prostrate lord below. "Who is that pale looking man?" says another. "Oh, that's J—— ——, of New Orleans—a great banker and capitalist." "And that dark man?" "Oh! that's a great slave-holder!"—and so on. I have several games of cards with two officers of the —, and the tragedian. The latter is full of anecdote and quotation.

Sunday turns out a beautiful calm day. A notice of divine service is posted up in the cabin, and at half-past ten the congregation begin to assemble. The sailors, dressed in their holiday blue jackets, occupy one end of the saloon, and the captain, assisted by the surgeon, begins the service, which is read very well. When it is concluded, the Captain asks the Unitarian minister to deliver a discourse, which he does in a simple straightforward way, avoiding every point that might be offensive to any one's individual opinions, and then gives out the Old Hundredth. It is some time before any one volunteers to lead. In this dilemma, I thought mournfully of poor Wilson, who had led the same psalm but a few months before, on his voyage across the Atlantic to the land, from which he was destined never to return. At length a little Scotchman begins,—the sailor who leads the chorus when the anchor is weighed, chimes in, —and the Old Hundredth is fairly got through.

The principal feature of Monday was a game called "The Knout," which has given rise to a great deal of fun and a great many tumbles on the quarter-deck. A flirtation which is watched with much interest, has sprung up between the funny man and the young lady, one of an Italian Opera *troupe* on their road to New York. Another of the passengers had set his affections there, but has been entirely cut out, and has shut himself up in his cabin ever since.

Tuesday was a nasty blowing sort of day, the sea very high and the passengers very low, and all right anxious to get to Halifax, which we hope to reach by 12 A.M. to morrow. Towards evening, however, the flirtations go on vigorously, in spite of wind and weather. The latest bulletin about the Republican (who had an attack of pleurisy) proves highly favorable, and the Post-office agent, a superannuated navy lieutenant goes round to collect all letters from the passengers.

CHAPTER II.

"Where Atlas flings his shadow,
Far o'er the Western foam."—*Macaulay.*

ARRIVAL AT HALIFAX—BOSTON AND ITS ENVIRONS—ITS HOTELS AND CEMETERY—NEW YORK—SCENERY ON THE HUDSON—THE AMERICAN MILITARY COLLEGE—VISIT TO THE KAATSKILL MOUNTAINS.

On Wednesday morning, the passengers all got up at a very early hour to hail the first glimpses of America. Breakfast was over before any thing very definite could be made out, on account of the fog, but that soon "lifted up," and we saw a curious sort of red barren coast extending for miles without any appearance of an harbour. In an hour or two, however, the land opened, and as we entered a splendid broad bay, we could see little white houses dotting the beach. The head-lands soon become more marked, lighthouses and ships loom into sight, another turn brings us at once amongst docks, wharfs, and houses, and we are once more safe on dry land. The postmaster, who has by this time become quite another man, and scarcely to be recognized in the immense cocked-hat with which he has invested himself, informs us with great dignity that we have an hour and an half to spend on shore, at which notice all the passengers took off and scampered over the town with the delight of school-boys. Halifax itself is not an interesting place, and only kept in being by the presence of two depôts of regiments of the line, and one of artillery. All the people about it have thoroughly English faces, and greet one with a thoroughly English accent. The wooden houses are nevertheless built in defiance of all straight lines and rules of order, and conjointly with the numberless negroes and grotesque carts go far to dispel the illusion. When, too, one climbs the ramparts and views the face of the surrounding country;

which is nothing more or less than miles of barren rocks, covered with low red underwood, one is immediately sensible of the great difference and contrast between the two countries. All the soldiers, curious as it may appear, have been transformed into "navvies," and are to be seen setting in motion some hundreds of wheels-barrows and spades with a view to building ramparts, works which have been going on for some years and which will be when finished, the most magnificent things of the sort in America. An heavy shower of rain interrupted us in our rambles, and our fellow passengers had to fly to all sorts of curious places for shelter. At last we all got back to the ship and set off for a 36 hours voyage to Boston, sailing against the wind all that afternoon. By midnight on Thursday, we were navigating with a fine clear moon to aid us among several little islands that cluster round the entrance to the Bay, and got safely moored in Boston harbour by half-past ten on Friday morning. The sun shone splendidly on Boston when we went on deck, and the gladdening view of a magnificent bay, noisy wharfs, and a town of all the colours of the rainbow spread out before us, made us well-nigh forget that there was such an institution as the Custom House, and such articles as luggage to pass through it, before we got any breakfast. That ceremony of examination occupied about an hour, and we then bade adieu to the steamer and got into a terribly jolting coach, overladen with luggage, and were knocked about over stones and against carts till we were set down at an hotel, which my weak mind conceived at once to be some splendid palace, at which we were to be boarded and lodged for eight and sixpence a day. We had breakfast in the most magnificent room I ever breakfasted in, about 90 feet long and proportionably high. The people seated themselves in two rows, and commenced sweeping off rolls, ham, and all sorts of delicacies at a very rapid rate, and I was not long in following their example. Somewhat sour bread and questionable milk for a fortnight, makes one thoroughly enjoy a comfortable terra-firma breakfast. I then went out for a stroll about the town, along with the tragedian

C

and a young English officer. It is one of the brightest and smartest you can possibly conceive. From the top of the States-House or Town Hall, there is a panorama-like view of the town and country for miles round, and among the most prominent objects stands the Bunker's Hill Column, at which every Englishman looks with a sigh. I will tell you some more particulars when I am here again, which will, I hope, be in about a month's time. There are three hotels here all of equal splendour, to wit the Tremont House, Rereu House, and the Albion, at each of which there is an immense ordinary at half-past two daily, when the table is laid out in a way that is perfectly marvellous. In every glass there is a napkin in the form of, and as white as a lily, and as there are four rows of perhaps sixty glasses each, the appearance exceeds anything I ever saw in the way of table-cloth effect, nor does the outward show surpass the reality. The hotel I am in can accommodate five hundred people. There are private dining-rooms and drawing rooms all furnished with pile carpets, massive furniture, and damask silk hangings. Each person is furnished with a key of his bed-room, and always locks up his room when he quits it, depositing the key in the bar. On Saturday morning J—— and I got up at seven, took a gig and drove round the town through the prettiest suburbs I ever saw, and so reached the Mount-Auburn Cemetery. This is one of the principal features of the place. It is entered by some gigantic gates, and we drove through it at a walking pace, keeping of course to the avenue from which numerous winding walks diverge, dignified by the floral names of "The Cypress," "The Harebell," "The Acacia," &c. There is no appearance of elaborate ornament about the tombs. Out of a grove of cypresses or shumachs you may here and there see some broken pillar or unostentatious urn, with the trees bending over and nearly shrouding them. The effect at this season of the year when the trees are just turning, and displaying every imaginable colour (except blue) from a bright yellow to a deep scarlet, is very softening and harmonises beautifully with the quiet scene of mortality. We left Boston and its attractions on Saturday evening, and travelled all night to New York, where we arrived somewhere about eight o'clock in the morning. The entrance to the Bay is considered very fine, but every thing was shrouded in fog. The day eventually cleared up, and turned out perfectly hot, in fact, an Indian summer day, of which I hope to see many more on my way North. The heat of the weather on the Sunday, and the heavy rain on Monday, prevented me from seeing much of the town at this visit. I am disappointed in the Broadway, which is about three miles long, but not so handsome as Piccadilly. I went to hear the best preacher there, Dr. Hanks, and a right eloquent and powerful discourse we had. The ladies as far as I can see, are handsome above the average. To-morrow at seven, I start in a steam-boat up the Hudson on my way to Niagara.

I can scarcely describe my feelings when I found myself at seven o'clock this morning, as clear and glorious a morning as I could wish to see, sailing up the Hudson, the river of which I have read so much, whose every rock, mountain and headland stands out as the hero of some fearful legend, or as the scene of some real and more stirring drama, in which English, American, and Dutch blood has been spilt like water, in defending wives and homes from Indian aggression hundreds of years ago, or in struggling gallantly to establish independence in nearly our own times. The first sight of this river convinces you that it stands unrivalled among all hitherto discovered rivers. Its width varies from eight hundred yards to two miles, and it winds its way through the most varied style of country. First, after leaving the ships and the nautical bustle of the Island of the Manhattoes, are to be seen the Palisadoes, a precipice or rather a series of precipices, which tower to a height of from fifty to an hundred feet along the left bank, till they are lost in the Bay of Tappaan or Tappaan Zee, the crossing-over of which by the heavy sterned Dutch settlers of former times, was thought to be the perfection of navigation. So tremendous were the visional terrors connected with this passage, that before undertaking it, each burgomaster used to make his will, and take a last farewell of his vrouw and chubby offspring. Passing through the bay, you find yourself surrounded by the Highlands, the great ornament of the Hudson, and beautiful they are in this season. They are not mountains of heather like their Scotch namesakes, but rugged precipices rising almost perpendicularly out of the water, and covered with lumps of rock and low red underwood. The most prominent of them is St. Anthony's Nose, called so as much from the colour which is unusually red, as from the shape, which is supposed to be a fac-simile of the nasal ornament of a certain Dutch trumpeter, who was more celebrated for blowing his own than his country's trumpet, and whose assiduities in this line thus found a reward after death. I must here remark that if the steam-boat in which I traversed the river were transported bodily into the Thames, a steam-boat is about the last name by which it would be called. To any eye accustomed to the beautiful proportions of an English steam-boat, an American one is a great mystery, a thing in fact that takes an inexperienced traveller a whole voyage to understand. Seen from the outside, it appears like a number of white galleries piled one on the top of the other. On the summit of all a great black engine shaft is working away, surrounded by a number of long poles surmounted with brass knobs. By looking carefully, you may discover two black chimnies, not in the place you look for them in a regular steam-boat, but here, there, and everywhere; sometimes in the middle, sometimes in the stern, or "forward." There is, in fact, no symmetry, no mast, no steersman, and no captain on the paddle-box; yet this indescribable monster goes along at the rate of from fifteen to twenty miles an hour, and furnishes a capital breakfast, dinner, supper, and bed, with all the convenience and elegance of an English hotel, and at a decidedly cheaper rate. In about an hour from the time we lost sight of the Highlands, it landed us safely at West Point, where I made up my mind to stay and see the Military College, the Sandhurst and Woolwich combined of the American forces. The college is a widely-extending well-built stone edifice, and the cadets, all dressed in grey uniforms, were busily engaged in field practice when I arrived. I went to the superintendent's office, a Captain something, and one of the mildest and yet finest-looking military men I ever saw. He at once introduced me to a young lieutenant who shook me cordially by the hand, and offered to show me all over the college. I went to it, I confess, rather puffed up with the superiority of the British military in general, and of British officers in particular, and disposed to look with complacency and indulgence on the war-like efforts of the young republic, but the gentlemanly bearing of this dignified old captain (I had set him down for a general at least), and his handsome young lieutenant made me look with much greater respect on republican warriors. The students are here instructed in every branch of the profession, as well as in classics, modern languages, and general drawing. A room full of their copies of Edwin Landseer's and a great many of Horace Vernet's pictures, testified the progress which the prizemen of each year had made in the latter art, while masters and a library of forty thousand volumes, to which the cadets have constant access, bring the three former within their reach. The lieutenant was extremely affable and explained everything. He was a great disciple of Vauban, Louis Fourteenth's celebrated general, and looked upon him as the grand master of fortification and gunnery, but did not say much when I suggested the Duke of Marlborough and Prince Eugene, and inquired how Vauban and his tactics got on in the Flemish campaigns of these two warriors. There was a court-martial that day, and a number of officers had congregated about the college. Some of them came into the inn and told stories about the Mexican war over the fire at night. One of the colonels impressed me strongly with the idea of what Johnny F——r, of L——te, would be if he could be induced to appear as a militia-man. They untied their waistcoats, chewed tobacco, and threw aside their dignity altogether. I joined the steamer that night, and had the advantage of a clear atmosphere and a magnificent moon all the way to Kaatskill, where I slept. The

Kaatskill mountains lie on the left of the Hudson. They are extremely famous for the view they command from their summits, but more especially for being the spot where Rip Van Winkle, a name dear to all lovers of American legends and Washington Irving, met Hendrick Hudson and his goblin crew, and slept his twenty years sleep. Not liking to miss this great feature of American scenery, I was off early for a ride of fourteen miles each way to explore them, as well as the beautiful falls in the neighbourhood. The way lay through a tract of country replete with thoroughly American scenery—bold, bare, and rocky. Here and there a comfortable wooden farm-house presented itself, seemingly well stocked with cattle, and showing every appearance of "well-to-doism." Sometimes the road wound through a plantation, which looked exactly like a badly-kept gentleman's grounds. The Hemlock fir, a beautiful evergreen, with its clusters of dark blue berries, seemed to be the predominant tree. Here and there a stream had broken loose and flooded the road, through which my driver urged his floundering nags in the best way he could. A church, too, built of white wood, and well-steepled and weathercocked, would start up here and there, and I looked eagerly round for some signs of a congregation, but could descry nothing but barren fields and plantations. At length we reached the foot of the mountains, and had to pursue for three miles a winding course, up their nearly perpendicular sides, through a splendid plantation, or rather forest of maple, which now and then opened out, and gave us glimpses of the treat in store. When we gained the summit, the weather was very fine and warm, and the ceaseless hum of locusts and grasshoppers, only relieved by the whistle of the quail, or the tapping of the woodpecker, was extremely novel and pleasing. The Mountain House is an immense hotel, full of galleries and green shutters, and situated at the very summit of the Kaatskills, but as the season is over, the galleries are tenantless and the shutters all closed. We drove up to the back door, where an hideous old negress received us and offered to cook my dinner. She is the only person in the house, as the proprietors, I suppose, think that she is ugly enough and strong enough to scare the thieves away. I postponed my dinner till I had seen the Falls, but first went to survey the prospect from the top of the hotel. I had come prepared for great things, and I was not disappointed. The extent over which I looked is not more than the eye can command from the highest mountains in Britain, but the colour, the different patches of colour, here and there marked so distinctly, here and there blended so delicately and imperceptibly into one another, the yellow into the red, the red into the brown, the brown into the dark blue, and the blue into the distant fleecy clouds, formed the elements of a picture, which Lee or Creswick could scarcely have realized. The Falls were much on a par with those of the Clyde; the principal one was perhaps a little higher, and owing to the great projection of the rock over which the water is hurled, one is able to walk right under it. After a scramble of three miles through the woods, where I lost myself once, and had unpleasant ideas suggested of wild cats and rattle-snakes, which are still to be seen in these regions, I managed to get back to the inn, and found the negress with a quantity of tough beef-steak and a lean chicken ready and smoking. At first I fell to lustily, but the meat had been fried in questionable butter, and unpleasant ideas would suggest themselves as to the part those horrid flabby fingers had played in the formation of the pumpkin pie, and I was therefore soon satisfied, and right glad to get away from my dusky Mrs. Glasse and her dismal abode.

CHAPTER III.

"And Airey Force, that torrent hoarse,
Speaks from its wooded glen."—*Wordsworth.*

AN AMERICAN TEMPERANCE MEETING—THE INN AT SARATOGA—THE STATE PRISON AT AUBURN—FOREST SCENERY—RAILWAY MANAGEMENT—NIAGARA—BATTLE OF LUNDYS LANE—VIEW OF THE FALLS FROM TABLE ROCK—VISIT TO A WAX-WORK EXHIBITION—A NATURAL SHOWER BATH—LORD ELGIN—INTERVIEW WITH A CANADIAN FARMER—QUEENSTOWN.

On my return from the mountain, I found the inhabitants of the usually apathetic village of Kaatskill almost beside themselves. The great Mr, Gough, second only to Father Mathew as a popular temperance lecturer, had suddenly signified his intention of appearing amongst them, and numerous bill stickers and criers were in motion to inform them of the same. I followed in the general stream and soon found myself in the principal meeting-house of the village, in which were assembled a large miscellaneous audience, but all quiet and attentive. When a prayer had been offered up by a precentor, and a sort of Gregorian chaunt had been performed by a juvenile choir, the hero of the evening, a quiet unpretending-looking young man began his address. At first he went on calmly and quietly, in a way really calculated to make proselytes not followers only, but soon the lion began to roar, and then he poured forth such a stream of noisy anathemas at the head of all hotel-keepers who sold anything stronger than tea,—such improbable anecdotes, such imprecations and groanings, interspersed here and there with bits of colloquial illustration, as quite astonished me. At one moment the audience would be aghast at some-appalling well-told tale of alcohol, and at the next, perfectly convulsed with laughter at some comic dialogue between Jehu and Sambo, two negroes, desirous of abjuring spirits, illustrated with all the action and modulation of voice, which we are accustomed to hear in the Ethiopian Melodist entertainments. Thus he went on for an hour and a half, and I confess he made me laugh very much, and I left the meeting with much the same feelings that a comic actor in a farce would have excited in me. The man had the power as an orator of doing great good to the cause, a cause which deserves much better encouragement than roars of laughter. I left Kaatskill late at night, and had all the beautiful Hudson scenery by moonlight again, and arrived at Albany on Thursday, about five o'clock in the evening. Albany is a large growing sea-port town, with some handsome hotels and public buildings, and I intend to re-visit it on my return south. I had been advised to see Saratoga, the Harrogate cum Cheltenham of America, a place crowded in the season by all the most fashionable people, not only of America, but (as the hotel-keeper pompously remarked) of the world. With that view, therefore, I got into a railway carriage for a ride of forty miles. I must say that I like the American car, in some respects, better than the English. It is about twice the length of an English carriage, and open all the way along, with seats to hold two persons ranged down each side, and a passage down the middle. In the centre is a stove, which keeps every one very comfortable except the person who may be forced to sit near it, as the Americans all chew, and the stove in a railway car is their spitting aim. The powers of expectoration are developed very early in Americans. I saw a little boy the other day very respectably dressed, sitting by his mother, a very lady-like-looking woman, and busily engaged in chewing a bit of wood, and playfully propelling particles of it and other substances all over the carriage, while his parent calmly watched the infantine shower, and seemed rather proud than otherwise of her son's accomplishments. After a long ride I got to Saratoga Springs, which I am told boasts of larger hotels than any place in America. One of them, the United States Hotel, holds 1,000 people, another 800, two or three 500, but now all these many-windowed palaces are closed for the season, and I had to content myself with the Adelphi, a seventh-rater,

D

but still conducted strictly on the American system. Behind the bar sat a spectacled landlord presiding over a mysterious well-worn book in which I was requested to enter my name, and then with all due dignity I was presented with the key of my bed-room, No. 6. There were only five more and none of them engaged, and I observed that the last visiting entry had been made ten days before. I was waited on by a dirty looking maid, who after she had served me, sat down right opposite to me at the table and dispatched her own tea and bread. I arrived at Auburn the next night, after traversing three or four lines, and made up my mind to stay and see the State Prison. I don't know what Goldsmith would have said with his ideas of rural innocence and purity, at his "Auburn, loveliest of the plain," furnishing a name for a State Prison, in which all the crime of a hardened community is congregated. But "What's in a name?" it sits as easily on a paradise as a prison! The system is an improvement on Pentonville. Instead of working gloomily in their own cells, not seeing a face but their keeper's, the prisoners all work together in large airy rooms. They are certainly not allowed to speak, but they see others near them in the same plight, and visitors come round every hour, and they work all the more cheerfully and better for this constant excitement. I was perfectly astonished at the phrenological development of some of the prisoners' heads; in fact I saw very low foreheads except amongst the blacks, who certainly did look villains every inch of them. They are taught weaving, spinning, machine-making, and carpentering, and some of them learn their trade in a few months. Thus they are taken into prison without a character and leave it with a trade; they are taken in vagabonds and go out useful members of society. Would that such a system could be carried out in England, but it is here that a new rising State has the advantage. It has no old prejudices to combat, no old interests to serve. Their motto is "Every one for himself," and the state, unfettered by the monopolies and drawbacks which exist in all long-established monarchies, adopts the motto and acts upon it. The line of railroad from Auburn, westward, is the most beautiful I have as yet travelled on. The country hitherto had been dull and uninteresting, but I now passed through a succession of highly cultivated fields and splendid forests. The train would now and then dash almost through a farm-yard, whose white and red barns were glowing in the afternoon sun, now it would skirt some lordly forest of pine and maple trees, nearly stripped of their leaves, it is true, but exhibiting more clearly on that account their massive trunks and twisted sinews. Here and there the forest would break, disclosing a long vista of green, which looked so park-like and thoroughly English, that I expected to see starting from it the "Gothic shade" or Grecian front of some ancient castle or modern mansion; but another illimitable forest succeeds, and I was in America again. It soon began to grow dark, and I tried to get something out of my next neighbour, but he was more inclined for sleep than talk; indeed I have come to the conclusion that the Americans are fast losing their characteristics, as I have not yet met with a genuine inquisitive Yankee. I went fully expecting to be bored with questions wherever I travelled, but I have hitherto found them unusually saturnine. What I admire as much as anything is their management of railways. They have no policemen, no gates, no expensive stations. A train rattles through the main streets of a town; carts, horses, and old women passing and repassing without any accident. When an engine moves in a station, it is generally attended by a lot of little boys clinging on behind and shouting. Fancy such a thing in Euston Square! When a public road crosses a railway, a simple board, with "*Look out for the cars when the bell rings,*" is put up across it, and supplies the place of a stone cottage, expensive gate, and blue-coated official, and yet you scarcely see a railway accident in the papers. Just let such a thing be done in England, and the papers would teem with old women run over, children killed, and carts overturned, and yet people are not considered more stupid in England than America. There is no doubt that this is one of the causes of the eight and twelve per cent. dividends which are commonly paid on these lines. At length we pulled up at Buffalo, after passing through the strangest medley of names—names classical, names poetical, names English, and names Indian. Fancy a person travelling in three hours from Rochester to Syracuse!—both large towns, and termini of a railway. Then we have Attica, Utica, Buffalo, Schenectady, Saratoga, Auburn—all large towns on the same line of railway. Who in the world ever christened them? I got a very uncomfortable bed at Buffalo, and a bad sprain in my knee into the bargain, and was therefore very glad to leave it and come to Niagara, where I spent the day rubbing in liniment and contemplating the falls, which send up such a cloud of foam as to wet the very window at which I sit. Hence I have only seen the general view of the falls, without exploring those fearful places among the rocks, where the bystander looks on in dreadful propinquity to the scene, stunned by its thunder and drenched by its foam. The view I have at present fully comes up to my expectations. I see both the falls, the American and the Horse Shoe, at a distance of about 500 yards, so you may fancy that my eye frequently wanders from the white paper to the white foam; and my ideas, instead of flowing gently from the end of my pen, and developing themselves quietly on the paper, are continually being borne down the rapids and over the cataracts, and are consequently in rather a mangled and unsatisfactory state when they are picked up again. It really is impossible to find words equal to the task of describing Niagara. All the high-sounding adjectives and adverbs our language affords have been expended over Lodore, Falls of the Clyde, &c. but have found it quite as much as they could do to do justice to the scene; so that when we come to a thing fifty times as fearful and fifty times as grand as any of them, language naturally gives in dead beat. I staid at Niagara four or five days, and after copious applications of opodildoc, which seems as efficacious in America as in the old country, I got quite right again. It takes fully four days of fine weather to thoroughly see Niagara and its neighbourhood, for the falls are far from being the only things of interest. There are rapids above the Falls, where logs, ships, human beings, and in short anything floatable is hurried along at the rate of twenty miles an hour. There are the rapids also below the Falls, where the current is deeper and stronger, and fenced in by crags 200 feet high, on which rests the suspension bridge. In its formation a small kite served to draw over a small string, that string a small rope, the small rope a larger one, and so on till at last the present magnificent structure was reared, which is the wonder and pride of both Yankees and Canadians. There is also a whirlpool, described in the guide book as producing the same sensations as are experienced by travellers to the great Norwegian Malstroom. In the neighbourhood is to be seen the battle field of Lundy's Lane, where a vast band of English and American soldiers fought from noon till dusk. Each claimed the victory, and with a considerable show of justice, for on inspecting the field of battle, foeman lay by foeman each transfixed by each other's bayonet, or clasped shoulder to shoulder for a fatal death-wrestle. We claimed the victory on the ground that the enemy retired during the night, which they did only to hurl their dead comrades over the Falls, so as to be enabled to boast of their lesser number in the morning. In this they were foiled, as the mangled corpses striking here and there on the rocks, and whirling round and round among the eddies for many a long day afterwards, before they took the last plunge in the whirlpool, sufficiently belied their assertion. Two high pillars, from the top of which garrulous old veterans retail the particulars of the fray at 6d. per head, serve to commemorate the spot. All these and minor objects of interest I visited during my stay, and as the visit to each involved a ramble through American forests overgrown with the beautiful hemlock-fir of this country, and swarming with woodpeckers and large black sqirrels, you may fancy that I passed my time agreeably. I was generally accompanied by two young fellows, one called G——, aide-de-camp to Lord Elgin, and the other a —— man, who has arrived to try a life in the Bush. He is possessed with a remarkable mania for cock-fighting, and looks forward confidently to the happy time when he shall have come into his fortune, and revived cock-pits in various towns in England. These two, with myself, and now and then a chance traveller passing through on his road to Buffalo, formed our dinner party daily in an inn, made to hold 400 persons, from which fact you may judge that I am a little behind the season. The most magnificent view of the Falls is obtained from the Table Rock on the Canada side, where you are within only ten feet of the Great Horse-shoe Fall, which is the principal one. Here you may stand for hours on a fine day, and never become tired of gazing. There are new beauties to be seen every minute, as the foam is ever changing its shape. Now it darts up in an enormous column, towering hundreds of feet above the highest points of the rocks—now it gets wafted by the wind into your face, and all over you, shrouding the Falls and the surrounding objects entirely from your view—now it is whirled off in another direction and goes right down the river, clinging for an instant to the top of the rocky bank in broad belts, before it is dissolved in air, and then perhaps the sun will dart out from behind a cloud, and instantly gossamer bridges of every shape and every hue of the rainbow, over which Queen Mab and her Pixy Court might have asserted their right, are thrown across the stream; then as they disperse, lovely-coloured spray-wreaths are to be detected flitting over the cataract, till they are lost again in the vast world of waters, only till the next gleam of sunshine brings them out as bright and beautiful as ever. The opposite side of the river is very much liked, but Table Rock is most famous, and after seeing the Falls from every possible point of view I must coincide in the latter opinion. It is a curious fact, that whatever substances float over the Falls are found eventually at one spot, about three miles down. I was told that a vessel, freighted with all kinds of animals, was once launched for a trial, and that the only thing which escaped with life, was a bear which was found at this spot, deliberately licking its paws in the midst of its dead comrades. Along the banks are various little marts for the sale of Indian curiosities, fashioned by the neighbouring tribes. At one of them is an excellent museum of stuffed animals, and some wax-work figures as large as life. I was introduced to several popular characters, including Columbus, Cassidy and Brooks (a brace of American "Rushes"), Lord Byron's Maid of Athens, and the Witch of Endor. All of these the showman assured me were admirable likenesses, especially the latter-mentioned one! Attached to this establishment is a small menagerie, where a splendid wolf acts as house-dog, and allows himself to be patted at discretion. I observed two buffaloes from the Rocky Mountains, the most hideous looking creatures, and a variety of smaller indigenous animals. Here also I confided my person to the care of a trusty black, who forthwith equipped me in a red flannel jacket, canvass trowsers, and an oil-skin cap, with a view to treating me with a shower-bath under Table Rock. A truly regal shower-bath it was. You walk right underneath the rock, and as the water comes thundering down over your head, you are so completely enveloped in mist that you cannot at times (amid the awful thunder of the waters), even see the Rock which you are grasping to save yourself from death. All these terrors, however, could not prevent me from laughing at the appearance of my sable guide, who was frantically endeavouring to express his ideas on the subject in a species of wild pantomime, or rather Ethiopian dance, which was also intended to illustrate the way in which a drunken man had slipped down from the rocks some months previous, and been dashed to pieces in his descent. I had a letter of introduction to Mr. B——, an ex-consul who resides here, whom I found in his shirtsleeves, and spectacles on nose and mallet in hand, busily engaged bottling a pipe of port. He was most kind and pleasant, and his son was my pioneer in a few walks. Lord Elgin is staying here now, right glad I should think to exchange the unsavoury eggs, cabbage-stumps, and hootings of Montreal mobs for the roar of Niagara waters. His aide-de-camp's lips are of course sealed, but I have not as yet heard a single person in Canada attempt to defend his conduct. He passed me on the road, riding out with his little daughter, and reminds me very much of Mr. G——ie, though he has perhaps more marked features. I left this place for Toronto on Lake Ontario, and had on my way thither to get into a sort of railroad, where three horses did duty for an engine, and found myself seated in a second class carriage with two soldiers' wives, seven children, two parrots, a canary bird, and a Canadian farmer. The latter was a most amusing fellow, and had taken under his care the whole of the former travellers, birds included, and behaved to all with equal attention and politeness. Having got out of me that I came from England, he then asked me if I knew such a place as B——n. I said I rather believed I did. He then told me that his name was E——, and that his father, who used to be a tailor there, had come out to America with 100 dollars in his pocket, got rich by farming, and had given himself and his brothers 100 acres of land a piece. He then emphatically added that he did not care two-pence for any body or any thing, and that he had just been out for a lark at Buffalo. After he had enquired my name, he became excessively familiar, and expounded to me all his private concerns, habits, and opinions, and demonstrated by a tremendous menace of his fist at the parrot opposite, the way in which he or any other Canadian farmer would "serve out them annexationist fellers," if they came near him. He then wound up his attentions by lugging me forcibly out of the carriage to share in some brandy, which he procured at a railway store. After about an hour and a half's ride, we got to Lake Ontario (Cooper's "Inland Sea"), and embarked at Queenstown for Toronto. At Queenstown, there is a monument to the memory of General Brock, who fell fighting against the Americans in the last war. A few years ago some wretched creatures attempted to blow it up, and succeeded in striking down the top and making large openings up the sides, but the form of the structure is still preserved.

CHAPTER IV.

And now a future opens o'er the sea,
In a new land where teems a virgin soil:
Where every pair of hands will welcome be,
And life is lightened with a hopeful toil.

Mrs. Loudon.

TORONTO—ITS MARKET PRICES—KINGSTON—THE "THOUSAND ISLES" OF THE ST. LAWRENCE—SHOOTING THE RAPIDS—MONTREAL—A BREAK DOWN—APPEARANCE OF QUEBEC—ITS MARTIAL RECOLLECTIONS—A PASSENGER GROUP—TRAVELLING TROUBLES—BOSTON—A POLICE OFFICE—LOWELL COTTON MILLS—A LUNATIC ASYLUM—AN EVENING PARTY.

AFTER some four hours sail over a stormy part of the lake, I arrived at Toronto, the future seat of government in Canada. On the pier I caught a last glimpse of my B——n friend, with two parrots under one arm and a baby under the other, helping the women and children to find the canary bird, which had suddenly disappeared. After going to six inns and finding them all full, I lighted at last on a public-house in a back street, where I was told that I could be accommodated with a bed in a double-bedded room, which, as it was late and a cold wet night into the bargain, I thankfully accepted, and never slept sounder, though at first my fellow-lodger disturbed me with his snoring. Toronto is a thoroughly English town, and all built of solid limestone, thus presenting a great contrast to the red and white houses I had seen for the last fortnight. It can boast of Yonge Street, a part of the longest "street" in the world, which extends for forty miles to Lake Simcoe. It has some excellent churches, and a large market, the best part of which is its cheapness. What think you of beef 3d. per lb. mutton 2½d., bread 1d., turkeys 2s. a piece, and chickens 1s. 6d. per pair? I must add that £1. 12s. is all the yearly tax which a man has to pay for a capital two-story house and a few acres of land. I soon left this for Montreal, and arrived the next morning at Kingston, after a most interesting sail. Kingston is the beau-ideal of a well fortified town, and has a battery which commands the whole passage from the Lake into the river St. Lawrence, which begins here. It would be almost impregnable in case of an assault, and as part of it stands on a large island, it would be very difficult to cut off its supplies. I intended to stay a day or so here, but as it poured with rain, the prospect was far from inviting, and therefore I thought it best to proceed. An hour's sail down the St. Lawrence brought us amongst the "Thousand Islands," and well do they deserve their world-wide fame. As far as the shape, variety of size, and beauty of them is concerned, they far surpass the islands in the Clyde. For four hours did our steamer pursue its winding way through these green patches, rocky it is true at the sides, but yet well covered with beautiful hemlock firs (which is, without exception, the most elegant evergreen I ever saw), and at times we were so thickly surrounded by them, that it became a perfect mystery to me how we were to get on; but then an opening would appear where I least expected it, and we could once more see the exact course of the river. Our passengers were few and very reserved, so that had it not been for the islands and the beautiful river-banks which are now and then separated by two hundred yards, now and then by two miles, and occasional stoppages at little bustling wharfs, where a large quantity of wood for the engine was shipped with a great deal of noise, I should have had but a dull day of it. At night we pulled up and moored our little vessel alongside a little jetty, and setting off soon after day break went through the first rapid. The sensation of being steamed and whirled along at the rate of five and twenty miles an hour is highly pleasant, and as we went through three of them during the day, the idea of danger soon vanished. At length we seemed to get into an inhabited country; little villas began to dot the banks, and at about two o'clock we came in sight of Lachine, from whence we took the rail to Montreal. The first thing that struck me at Lachine, was the frequent knots of French Canadians, who seemed to hang idly about, jabbering a sort of French *patois*, in which I could now and then detect some slang English expression. The contrast between these fellows and the English was very remarkable. I put up at the hotel at which poor G. F. died, and met one of my voyage acquaintances who had come here to be married. I was also introduced to Mr. ——, the editor of a newspaper. He had just been challenged by an English officer, and instead of retorting with pistols had done so with paragraphs, and these with the answers to them had furnished a great fund of amusement to the town. I was much pleased with every thing here, but I did not escape the sickness which the water generally produces in new-comers, and which laid me low for two long days. At length I got up and took a drive in company with Capt. C. round the Mountano, to a large wooded hill in the neighbourhood, from which a very good view of the town, with its two cathedral towers, each 250 feet high, may be obtained. It has several very handsome streets all built of white limestone, and its suburbs are principally composed of little French villas, all built with gable ends, and extremely pretty from their very irregularity. The roofs of the houses are generally made of tin, which, when seen from an eminence reflecting back the brilliant Indian sun, present a most dazzling appearance. It is a great place for Roman Catholics, and their priests attract the eye every moment from the strangeness of their dress and the meekness of their looks. During my sail from this place to Quebec, the steam-boat came to a stand-still in consequence of some accident to its engines, and I had consequently to stay all night at a little town called Sorelle. In the morning I heard that the engineer (a Frenchman), so far from repairing the engine, had not, after a night of profound meditation, discovered what was the matter with it. As I had therefore no hopes of getting to Quebec till the next steamer arrived, and as it was a glorious bright hoar-frost morning, I set off for a ramble into the country. I found that Sorelle is also called "William Henry," from a visit which was paid it some 50 or 60 years ago by our "Sailor King." It is a remarkably clean and highly coloured little place, the houses being red and white alternately, interspersed every now and then with a green one. Conspicuous amongst them all was a very large Roman Catholic chapel, built of massive grey stone. The outside of it, however, was somewhat tawdry, and the figure of the virgin was made of wax and attired in rather unbecoming spangled drapery. As it at length turned out that the piston rod of the good ship "John Munn," was hopelessly broken, our captain had to charter one (which had been laid up for eighteen months, with three feet of water in the hold), to take us on to Quebec, which we reached in safety about 9 a.m. after a sixteen hours' sail. The first view of Quebec from the river is most imposing. It is a city built on a hill, which rises almost perpendicularly out of the water. Its houses look as if they were placed one on the top of the other, and the weather-cocks and steeples in the lower part of the town seemed to rest against the windows of the houses above them; in fact the rules of perspective are quite set at defiance. The whole medley is surmounted by the fortress, which is considered to rank next to Gibraltar, *i. e.* of course, when defended by Englishmen. After a most laborious clamber up the steep hill, I got to the ramparts, from which is to be obtained a magnificent view of the St. Lawrence, winding along for a great distance on one side, and of innumerable white villages dotting a vast mountainous tract of country on the other. On the plains of Abraham, now a most unpretending turnip field, stands Wolfe's monument, lately erected, as the original one had been dreadfully defaced by sailors and other enthusiastic Englishmen chipping little pieces off it as relics. The present monument is a handsome stone pillar, on which is inscribed—"Here died Wolfe victorious, 1754." Not far from it is a monument to his great opponent, Montcalm. If I had had time I should have gone to see the falls of Montmorency, which are about four miles out of the town, and one of the villages where real Indians are still living in almost their original state, but I had lost a day on the St. Lawrence and I wanted to get south. We had quite a picturesque group of passengers on the forecastle of the steamer as we sailed back to Montreal. Canadians in rough grey coats, with their waists encircled with bright scarlet handkerchiefs and their feet encased in many-coloured mocassins, or long shiny boots, were mixed up with Yankees, Irishmen, and hideous-looking squaws, who were going to Montreal to sell their wares, dressed in blankets and extraordinary leggings, and each carrying a bundle or a child. This assemblage raised a perfect Babel of voices composed of bad French, guttural Indian, and Tipperary brogue. In going along we disturbed large flocks of wild geese and ducks; the latter are known by the name of "canvass-backs," and considered most delicious eating in Canada. On the banks of the river, the bells of the Roman Catholic Chapels were ringing, and carts and other vehicles were busily carrying their loads of church-goers. After dining at the mess of the 23rd at Montreal, I reached Burlington, and set off at two o'clock in the morning by a railway lately opened to Boston. As the only passenger van had broken down, we had to travel some sixty miles in a luggage car seated on our portmanteaus. However, one does not always require an arm chair in order to travel pleasantly. We had a gentleman (whom I used to know a little of in London) in the party, who had the happy knack of making the best of everything, and, in addition to a very fine day, the company of several young American ladies; and thus we managed, in spite of having to get out in a body more than once to collect wood for the engine fire, most thoroughly to enjoy ourselves, and I don't think that one of us (ladies included) would have exchanged our hard seats and mishaps for the cushioned ease of an English first class. We had also to coach, or rather cart it across country part of the way, half of us in a tremendous coach on gigantic springs drawn by six horses, and the other half in a sort of vehicle with a body composed of loose boards, which managed to transport us fourteen miles in something over four hours. At last we reached Boston, where I found my letters, and here I may as well mention that two thinnish sheets are the postal allowance. After leaving my letter of introduction on G. G.'s friend, Mr. H——, I sauntered into the police-office, which presented much the same scene as an English one. The only difference is, that witnesses hold up their hands when they are sworn, instead of kissing the book, and the prisoner, whether he stands charged with discolouring a friend's eye or picking a pocket, is gravely alluded to by judge, jury, and advocates as *Mr. So and So.* I went off early the next morning to have a day at Lowell, the Manchester of the United States. It, however, only resembles its great prototype so far as the trade is concerned; everything else about it is in strong contrast, and it seems the veritable fairy-land of factories. There is no smoke, water power being used universally, no dirt, no poverty, no wretchedness; every body every and thing else about it betokens happiness, cleanliness, and a full enjoyment of the comforts of this life. I watched a crowd of young work-people going to their dinner, and was perfectly astounded. Instead of the hatless and shoeless crowd which rattle along the streets of England with tin-cans in their hands, an orderly set of young ladies and gentlemen, the former dressed in smart shawls and visites, and worsted or straw bonnets with long green veils (one had a chatelaine), and the latter in Wellington boots, glazed caps, and Chesterfield coats, are to be seen sauntering homewards, conversing not in the language which would emanate from the lips of English piecers and winders, but on topics of deep interest, generally politics. I followed some of the girls, at a distance, to their lodgings, beautiful red brick houses of two stories in height, and caught glimpses of them through the windows. One of them positively laid aside her shawl, put on a light easy dressing gown, dropped into a luxurious arm chair, and began to con over a novel, while from another room I heard, almost simultaneously, the opening notes of a tune on the piano. These girls usually earn from 2½ to 5½ dollars per week (from nine to twenty shillings), and living is about half what it is in England. The population of Lowell is estimated at 35,000. There is a valuable library of

7,000 volumes belonging to it, to which any one can have access by paying fifty cents. (2s. 1d.) per annum. Its fire department is very efficient and well regulated —none can be more so. The facilities afforded for extinguishing fire by the rivers and canals running through the city, combined with the powerful action of the mills in forcing water almost everywhere, with the advantages also of its spacious streets, render it next to impossible for the most threatening fire to make much progress. The number of engines is 11, of firemen 745, and of feet of hose 17,410. Twenty cents. per hour is a fireman's pay. I went to church next day, at Boston, with Mr. V. to hear the Bishop of Eastburn preach, and a capital old orthodox sermon it was, doing full justice to the purple and fine linen from which it came. The organ at Trinity Church is considered to be the finest-toned in the States, and the singing was magnificent. On the Monday, I went to see the Lunatic Asylum, in the management of which institutions the Americans generally stand out in pleasing contrast to the "old country." Instead of the dingy looking buildings which disfigure the Knightsbridge-road, London, you enter a large and villa-looking sort of place, built on the top of a hill, which commands a view for miles such as the patients highly relish. The garden in which they walk is so arranged as to make the high wall which surrounds it, useful only as a safeguard, not as a barrier between them and the world, for there is to be seen from it, spread out at their very feet, a large bustling city with railways rattling to and fro directly beneath them, and ships gliding in and out of harbour in the distance. Inside, too, the arrangements are much on the same principle. The temperament of each of the patients is carefully watched, and they are all sorted in different companies, the members of which sit, read, work, and play at chess, back-gammon, and billiards together. I did not see one very painful case. One elderly lady certainly came up to me with a long letter, which she had written to her daughter, and wished to sell me it for a newspaper. She, in fact, dived boldly into my pocket to find one, but not being successful, placed the letter on a chair and danced round it, frisking off every minute into a pirouette. They seemed for the most part very cheerful, working or walking, and very few of them seemed to be labouring under that gloomy madness which baffles all skill. The keeper spoke in a sanguine way of all, and said he had very few incurables. All Boston was astounded during my stay by a report of the disappearance of Dr. Parkman, a man of great wealth and standing there, who left his family a week ago, and has never been seen since. Large rewards were offered, but nothing satisfactory could be heard of him, except that he had last been seen entering the walls of the Medical College on a visit to one Dr. Webster, who owed him some money. Dr. W.'s private room had been locked all the week, and dense columns of smoke had been observed issuing out of the chimney, an unusual thing, as the Dr. was never in the habit of locking up his room (a sort of laboratory) nor of having a fire in it. These odd facts roused the curiosity of a servant in the college, who was induced to break through a wall, and thus gain access to a cellar under the Dr.'s room, where he was horrified by seeing the mutilated remains of a human being. Upon this, the room above stairs was forced open, and the grate was found full of calcined bones and teeth stuffed with gold, which latter were recognized as belonging to Dr. Parkman. Dr. Webster was immediately arrested at his house in the country, and on being told the cause, fell into convulsions, and has remained in an almost insensible state ever since. On stricter search, the police found more of the body concealed up and down the room. Webster had nothing to do with the dissecting part of the establishment, which makes it more strange. The feeling about it is most intense, and it was with great difficulty that the mob were dissuaded from setting fire to the college. I went to an evening party at Mr. ——, and was right glad, after leading the life of a rover for seven weeks, to find myself once more conversing with a lady on a civilized ottoman. Late dinners are not known in America, and ponderous teas with sundry sweet accessories are substituted for them. The evening was an exceedingly pleasant one, and in the course of it we had fireside games and music. All the family seem musically inclined, the daughters played on the piano, and their father on the drum, while the son-in-law sang, and Mr. ——, jun. whistled.

CHAPTER V.

Men my brothers, men the workers,
Ever reaping something new;
That which they have done but earnest
Of the things that they shall do.
I doubt not that thro' the ages
Some increasing purpose runs,
And the thoughts of men are widened
With the process of the suns.

TENNYSON.

THE AMERICANS—THEIR MEANS OF TRANSIT—TAXATION IN CANADA—ANNEXATIONIST ARGUMENTS—THE LANCASTER MILLS—AMERICAN SERVANTS—A LITERARY SOIREE—MR. N. P. WILLIS VERSUS "LITTLE LIONS"—THE NEW YORK OPERA—NEW YORK AND ITS LADIES—THE BROADWAY—THE HOTELS—A BRITISH FESTIVAL—A NEGRO CHAPEL.

THE most apathetic traveller can hardly fail to be deeply struck with the Americans, for viewed in any light, or under any circumstances, they are truly a wonderful people. Whether he looks at their town of Boston, a large type of many cities of the same class, places but of yesterday, but now rapidly on the increase and swarming with all the elements of commercial wealth,—whether he travels along their immense channel of trade from New York to Buffalo, through which all the rich stores of the far west are poured in one continuous stream to supply the wants of an immense consuming population in New England, or to be shipped for the benefit of their more needy neighbours in the "old country;" or whether he looks on them in their individual character and sees their energy and their indomitable resolution of going a-head at any cost, which backed up by their extreme "coolness" and perseverance, baffles all opposition, he cannot fail to arrive at this conclusion. I am here speaking only of the people I have hitherto seen, the Americans of the

North, who are a different race from their southern brethren, and present a much better specimen of the Yankee character. What first struck me both in New York and Boston, is the way in which Nature has favoured them as regards harbours. As the deep water in their wharfs enables vessels, of from one to two thousand tons burden, to lie close up to their very streets and turn round and go out at any state of the tide, they have no wet and dry docks to build at an enormous expense, and hence the heavy dock dues and other legitimate taxes on shipping, incurred in an English port, are almost totally unknown. Their gigantic navigable rivers also, which run up into the interior of the country and are there joined to the continuous chain of western lakes (every bank of which is now fast being farmed and made productive), will always form the principal mediums of traffic; for railways, inexpensively as they are got up here, will never be able to rival them in cheapness. The towns and ports of Canada present a great contrast to all the marts of bustle and excitement in the northern parts of the States. Annexation or non-annexation, with invectives against Lord Elgin, are the principal topics of conversation there. The case is exactly the reverse of England, as every body complains of approaching ruin with the exception of the farmers in the west or Upper Canadians, who, as far as I could learn, are a pretty contented, very loyal and extremely independent race. They are mostly the sons of English settlers, who when they first came into the country had to buy a few acres of wooded land at from two to four dollars (8 to 16 shillings) per acre, which they cleared at the cost of about twelve dollars per acre. All the wood on it was of course their property, and if the land happened to be in the neighbourhood of a village, of considerable value for firewood. By degrees they bought more and more land, till they have now become men of some property. Their taxes are but light, and all their property is assessed in the following way, reckoning 4s. 2d. to a dollar:—An acre of uncultivated land pays one dollar, and one of cultivated, four; a horse pays eight and a cow six. Farm houses are assessed according to value. If the house has more than three fire places, it is assessed at three dollars. Other farming stock, except sheep, pigs, and fowls, which are very lightly assessed, are exempt from taxation. On all these assessments a further duty of 1d. in the pound is levied. They of course grumble at their neighbours over the boundary getting 4s. 6d. per bushel (60lb.) for their wheat, while they only get 2s. 9d. to 3s. yet they would not purchase this advantage at the expense of annexation, for in the first place they are afraid to compete with the Americans if they were subject to the same taxation, and they moreover detest the "Yankees" most cordially as a nation, and keep up all the feelings and loyalty of Englishmen. It is in the large towns and the eastern parts of Canada, where the population is very French, and where most of the people who were active in quelling the rebellion of 1836 reside, that the annexation question is so popular. They are generally native Canadians or English settlers engaged in trade as merchants and large storekeepers, who, although they live on the banks of the great vehicle of intercourse with the Old Country, the River St. Lawrence, yet find their American neighbours passing them at every stride, and British capital and enterprise, which they consider ought to be directed to them exclusively, going elsewhere, and consider the repeal of the corn and timber duties as a sure sign that England is forsaking them. The alteration of the navigation laws must do them a great deal of good, by creating competition, and a consequent reduction in the freight and insurance on the St. Lawrence, which is now enormously high from the difficulties of navigation, it being in fact cheaper to pay the 25 per cent. on Canadian wheat and send it through the States to England, than to send it duty free through their own native channel. Owing to the repeal of the timber duties, the Baltic has in a great measure cut them out of their trade in that article, but though very much stung by the fancied neglect of the old country and by the leading articles of the *Times*, which although much laughed at, is without doubt their real oracle, I think that the majority of Canadians very much dread annexation, and I have little doubt that if Lord Elgin were to be recalled to-morrow, and the duty on wheat into America taken off, very little more would be heard about annexation, independence, or anything else. Just before I left Boston I visited the Lancaster Mills. The work-girls there are all paid by the piece and earn, exclusive of board, from two to six dollars per week. They mostly come from farms about the country, and their parents are generally well off, so if they don't like the wages they get, they turn round and go quietly home, thus making themselves quite independent of the master. The boarding-houses here are on the same principle as at Lowell. The workpeople pay so much a-week for their board; and those who have families keep house and have all the necessaries of life—meat, bread, eggs, milk, &c.—brought out of the country by the farmers to their very doors, so that they are certain of having the best of everything without any trouble. I proceeded from Boston to New York, and was glad to have a week of comparative repose, after the twenty mile an hour excursion of the two previous ones. Living in hotels is much preferred by some of the best people here to the pains and penalties which assail them in housekeeping, especially in the servant line. The relation between master and man is a totally different thing to what it is in England. From the free and independent state of society in this country every body is allowed to be as good as every body else, and this idea is perhaps more strongly developed in servants than in any other class, for unless they are bribed by most enormous emoluments they will do exactly as much or as little as they like; they leave when they like, and are respectful or not as they like. They are hired by the month, and if their master does not suit them they can leave on the second day after their arrival and can demand wages for the whole time. The consequence is, that people must either have Ethiopian servants, or what is worse, Irish ones, or else give up housekeeping and betake themselves to hotels. The American coachmen are very original subjects. Instead of the powdered obesity and liveried dignity of our English hammercloth, you see a queer-looking man, with his legs (half of which are encased in long Wellington boots) stretched over the top of the splash-board, as if he was the sole owner of the carriage and every thing in it. A small carriage called a waggon, which is principally built with the view to showing off a horse's trotting powers, is the great fancy of young Americans. I went to stay at a Mr. S.'s country house, about six miles out of town, and was there introduced to his father, who has one of the best collections of pictures in New York. They were kind enough to take me to a literary reunion given by one Miss ——, an American authoress of some note, who always opens her house (N.B. Not the larder or cellar) on that evening, and to point out to me many of the notabilities in the New York world of letters. Many of them were real "lions," and not a few only wore the skin. The latter classes made themselves undesignedly very amusing, and were mostly little men, who had published and circulated a novel or two largely among their friends, which in their own opinions entitled them to turn down their shirt collars, allow their hair and beards to grow at random, and to assume the appearance of men in whom mind had become so predominant over body, as to render the latter quite a minor consideration. They did not open their lips all the evening, but were to be seen in pensive attitudes with their arms leaning on chimney pieces, and looking pleasantly at vacancy, or seated on solitary ottomans, contemplating the company with a sort of cynical stare. They wished in fact to be considered as living in an atmosphere of dreams, and nobody offered to disturb them. Mr. N. P. Willis, to whom I was introduced, afforded a very pleasant contrast to these little lions, and laughed and talked on many subjects like an ordinary being. Miss ——, too, has nothing of the pedant, and very little of the professed "blue" about her, and though on the verge of forty, wound up the amusements of the evening by gracefully leading off in a polka. During the evening a "hush" was circulated all round the room, and on enquiry I found that a Herr something, very like Puddlewitz, "was going to play his thoughts," and forthwith a foreign gentleman with as much hair as one face could conveniently carry, sat down at the piano. From the nature of the music, I should say that Puddlewitz's thoughts were of a remarkably mild and sentimental nature, and not at all in keeping with his ferocious aspect. After the polka, the little lions began to rouse themselves and to dispel the mental web, which their thoughts had been working round them for the last two or three hours, and we all gradually dispersed. Mr. S. asked me to his private box at the opera last week. There is no division of the boxes as in England, but the whole theatre is thrown open, as all such curtained seclusion is thought quite unworthy of a free and enlightened republic. By this arrangement, the appearance of the house is decidedly improved, as all the ladies and their brilliant dresses are exhibited to the view at once. The opera, as far as the performance and music goes, is quite a secondary consideration and vastly inferior to any thing in England. The first-rate artistes will not tempt the Atlantic when they can make handsome fortunes elsewhere; and the consequence is, that such phrases as "that love of a Mario," and "that dear old Lablache," are quite unknown, and the interest felt by the ladies in the performance naturally droops. The orchestra is equally inferior. For instance, when the tenor reduced to the very lowest depths of despair, has recourse to the highest pitch of his voice previous to stabbing himself, out comes the clarionet with an ebullition of feeling so loud and piercing, as totally to drown the voice and feelings of the unhappy suicide. As such unnatural ebullitions of feeling on the part of the wind instruments are of constant occurrence, one cannot wonder that opera glasses instead of being levelled at the stage, are turned by the spectators on to one another. Eager glances are directed through them to find "who's here and who is not,"—to see whether one of the ton here, is as much coloured to night as she was last,—to see how a distinguished beauty, who married some few weeks ago an immensely rich old man looks to night;—or who that handsome man with large moustaches is, who has stood in a corner all the evening. This sort of thing keeps up a regular hum in the theatre throughout the evening, and the music is emphatically "no where." The admission is very low and ranges from one to six shillings. New York is a town which depends for beauty much more on its situation and its environs, than on any grandeur or design in its streets and buildings. It stands on an island with two beautiful rivers on its north and east sides, the sea is on its south, and a little river running from south to north, flanks it on the west. Its population comprises 400,000 souls, and is rapidly on the increase. Indeed it is quite fearful to think what it will arrive at in 50 years time, in consequence of the number of the strangers who are perpetually settling in it, and the alarming fecundity of its inhabitants. Young ladies are put forward much more here than in England. As children they are the constant companions of their mothers, and at fourteen have generally all the air and manners of English debutantes. During their stay at school, they are allowed to go to parties and operas two or three times a week, marry from 17 to 19, become mothers, and by the time they are 30 have too often become pale and thin. But these young ladies have quite put the town out of my head. The Broadway is about as broad and reminds me very much of Oxford-street. It is the promenade of the town, and at three o'clock in an afternoon, presents a very animated scene. Gaily dressed ladies and black-bearded cavaliers are to be seen in scores, the former for the most part wending their way to Stewarts, the "Swan and Edgar's" of New York, which is really a most magnificent shop, or I should rather say, "store." Here the ladies are waited on by young men in black, as in London, but they have not by any means the same obliging manners, or polite bows, for being Americans, they consider themselves in every respect on a par with their customers and conduct themselves accordingly. Through two of the principal streets, a railway is laid down, along which two horses draw immense omnibusses calculated to hold sitting and standing about forty people. The railway cars, which are twice the length of ours, are on their arrival in the station yard unfastened from each other and drawn by four horses down this street railway into the middle of the city, where there is a passenger and goods depôt—a most convenient arrangement. In the hotels where nearly one half the American world pass the winter, the company all meet at a five o'clock ordinary, where acquaintances are very soon formed. There is no English reserve here, the greatest strangers become the greatest friends in two hours, though the depth and sincerity of such friendships I am somewhat disposed to doubt. The bed-rooms are all made exactly on the same plan, the beds being altogether destitute of posts and curtains; in fact a regular curtained English four-poster is not to be had in the States. The public rooms are finished on the most gorgeous scale. Hotel keepers are not satisfied with Brussels carpets, but have the most splendid soft pile ones, into which you sink your foot about an inch at every step, and the mirrors and tables are also got up, like the "dandy Broadway swells," perfectly regardless of expence. There are very few buildings in the city worthy of special notice. I must not, however, forget to mention a very splendid church, dedicated to the Holy Trinity, which has lately been built in the purely Gothic style. Its height is 284 feet, including the weathercock, and it is not painted but composed of light red sandstone most elaborately worked, with all the fancies which that style commands. About two miles off, is the Greenwood Cemetery, laid out in the same way as the Boston one, but much larger and situated on higher ground, so as to command an extensive view of the Narrows, Staten Island, Levy Island, and the mouth of the Hudson. I only saw it when snow was on the ground, but I could fancy that it must be a most enchanting place in summer. We Britons had quite a festival last night. A concert was given by the St. George Society, in aid of the fund for supporting and promoting the interests of poor emigrants from the mother country. We had "God Save the Queen" and some few English songs, but the star of the

G

evening was Fanny Kemble, late Mrs. Butler, who volunteered to read "As you like it." Of course this drew together an immense crowd of "Englishers," as they are called here, and the sight of so many broad British faces, whose origin beamed out in every lineament, in spite of the hideous beards with which many were disfigured, lighted up at the sound of our national anthem, was very pleasing and promotive of loyalty. Fanny Butler, the last of the Kembles, has always been a favourite in America, but the circumstances of her late divorce and the cause in which she was engaged, combined to make her reception most enthusiastic, and well did she sustain her reputation. The sight in the Steward's Room behind the scenes was very amusing. The English Consul was there along with a number of merry gentlemen, with orders on their breasts, signs of their evening's office, drinking champagne and indulging at intervals in little isolated scraps of "God save the Queen," for their own peculiar benefit. I was introduced to most of them by Mr. —— (who seems on intimate terms with every body) including the Consul and Mr. H. a friend of Mr. E. M.'s, who asked me most kindly to dine and stay at his house. Some joke with reference to myself at Mr. —— expence, excited such laughing and noise, that a special message was sent from the theatre to see what was the matter, and to beg silence, as the good fellowship behind the scenes was sadly interrupting some fantasia on subjects from Gulliaume Tell. Before I left New York I attended a negro class meeting, and was not at all prepared for the strange sight it afforded. A black preacher in a white waistcoat and black neckerchief occupied the pulpit, and after a hymn had been very fairly sung by the women, who sit quite apart from the men, this dark expounder began in a very mild impressive sort of way to explain a passage out of Kings, full of very hard Old Testament names. These he, however, managed to get over in a jumbled up sort of way, and by the use of Massah, as a sort of handle every now and then, and soon without any connecting link he began to descant on the equal right that poor black men had to be saved with rich white men. This theme worked up the feelings of his audience, and there ran through the meeting house a sort of seething or bubbling, interspersed at intervals with an explosive burst from some highly hysterical negress, which gradually increased with the intensity of the subject and the excitement of the speaker, till at last every body was howling, stamping, and ejaculating. An immense negro close by me raised himself to his full height, and lifting his hands above his head, roared out "Glory to God! Send the truth home! Lord save us or we perish! Hallelujah! Amen!" till he was obliged out of sheer exhaustion to sit down again. By this time the energy of the speaker had quite outstripped his powers of enunciation, and he only contrived to gasp out something quite unintelligible, which dumb show, however, seemed only to increase the ardour of his audience, and even when he had concluded, and the crowd were dispersing through the streets to their different homes the women still vented their over-excitement in most hideous yells and gesticulations. The house they met at was called the African Mission House, and I am told that an English preacher once lectured them severely from their own pulpit for these strange practices, and that they listened to his discourse and did not commit themselves once during the whole of it.

CHAPTER VI.

"Mr. Speaker: Sir,—Our fellow-citizen Mr. Silas Higgins, who was lately a member of this branch of the legislature, is dead, and he died yesterday in the forenoon. He had the browncreaters (bronchitis) and was an uncommon individual. His character was good up to the time of his death, and he never lost his voice. He was fifty-six years old, and was taken sick before he died at his boarding-house, where board can be had at a dollar and 75 cents a week, washing and lights included. He was an ingenious creatur, and in the early part of his life had a father and mother. His uncle Timothy Higgins served under General Washington who was buried soon after his death with military honours, and several guns were bust in firing salutes. Sir, Mr. Speaker,—General Washington would have voted for the tariff of 1846 if he had been alive, and hadn't a'died sometime beforehand. Now, Mr. Speaker, such being the character of General Washington, I motion that we wear crape around the left arm of this legislature, and adjourn till to-morrow morning as an emblem of our respects for the memory of S. Higgins, who is dead, and died of the 'browncreaters' yesterday in the forenoon."—*Florida Debates.*

ARRIVAL AT PHILADELPHIA—ARRANGEMENT OF THE STREETS—THE STATES HOUSE—THE BRITISH CONSUL—THE WATER WORKS—CHRISTMAS PRESENTS—CLERICAL EMOLUMENTS—AMATEUR FIRE SOCIETIES—AN AMERICAN JUDGE—AN IMPRISONED ARTIST—RAILWAY BRIDGES—EMANCIPATED SLAVES—WASHINGTON—THE STATES HOUSE PICTURES—A DEBATE—LEADING POLITICAL CHARACTERS—THE PRESIDENT'S LEVEE—SAIL DOWN THE POTOMAC.

On Friday, December 21, I began to be a rolling-stone again, and getting all my things collected, made a start for Philadelphia. I left at four in the afternoon, and crossed the beautiful mouth of the River Hudson in a ferry-boat, just as the sun was setting; and after a railway ride of four hours and a half, stopped on the banks of the Delaware River, where I got into a steam boat, which brought me to Philadelphia by ten. I put up at the United States Hotel, which is the best in the town, but like many other American hotels, pervaded by an undeniable smell of grease. I lost it altogether at New York; but here it started up again as bad as ever. On Saturday the rain came down in a way I have never yet seen. In fact, from seven to two, it poured without any intermission as heavily as it sometimes does in a twenty-minutes English thunder shower. Every body was driven out of the streets or rather street, as my view from the hotel was not very comprehensive, but by the afternoon, thanks to the clever sloping construction of the streets and pavement, and a good N.W. wind, every thoroughfare was passable and crowded again. Philadelphia is the capital of Pennsylvania, and was laid out by William Penn, and really no one but a Quaker would have performed the task in such a unique style. The streets are all as straight as a line could make them. In fact there is only one street that has the slightest pretentions to being crooked. The town is bounded on the east by the Delaware river; on the west by the Schuylkill (pronounced School-kill), and between these two rivers run a number of parallel streets, bearing the name of different trees, *i. e.* Chesnut-street, Vine-street, Walnut-street, Sassafras-street, &c. These are crossed by 1st street, 2d street, 3d, and so on to 12th, which is about the middle of the town, when they take the name of the Schuylkill, and are called Schuylkill 1st, 2d, 3d, and so on. This regularity makes it very easy for strangers to find their way, but very hard for them to remember the names or the numbers of the street. It is a very clean town, and many of the houses are faced with a very beautiful white marble which is found in the neighbourhood. A considerable number of the public buildings are built entirely of this stone, and glittering palaces they look. In the States House here, a sort of Hampton Court looking building, which is a refreshing contrast to so much newness and show, the declaration of independence was signed by Washington and his fifty-five companions and publicly proclaimed from the steps. The furniture here is preserved just as it was on that day, down to every little minutiæ, and will, I dare say, remain so for centuries, unless fire, which is very partial to Philadelphia, makes it its prey.

I presented my letters of introduction to Mr. F. and Mr. B. and received invitations from both. I dined with Mr. B. on two successive days, having received the second invite for the ostensible purpose of tasting some canvass-back ducks. I also called on the English Consul Mr. P. in whom I found a very kind old national guardian. He told me that he was a Cornwall man, and drew me out in no time a hurried sketch of what I was to see while here, and what was worth going into the country to see, offering at the same time to procure any number of tickets for any number of institutions, and any letters of introduction to superintendants of lunatic asylums, gaols, or houses of refuge. He knew every body, and any friend of his would be respected, and he would come and call to-morrow if it was fine and walk out with me, so you may fancy that I left his house highly delighted. I took a long walk with Mr. B. on the banks of the Schuylkill, which supplies all the town with water by means of some stupendous water works, by which the water is pumped up into immense reservoirs which command the tops of the houses. From these reservoirs, on the cleaning out of which numberless skeletons of animals are discovered, a very good view of the town is obtained, which is almost destitute of steeples, and has rather an odd appearance in consequence. On one side is the Gerard College, to build which £400,000. was left by one Gerard, a miser. The middle building of it is a splendid specimen of the Corinthian order, and each of its pillars cost £5,000. I found at Mr. B.'s a large family party suggestive of Christmas. The old grandmother of the party, who was about 90 years of age, would talk every now and then about "the late war!" She seemed quite pleased with being reminded that she had once been a British subject, and launched out about her young days with great gusto. It is quite the custom here amongst all classes to make very large Christmas presents. Children look forward to them as a matter of course, and old unmarried uncles are made to bleed pretty freely. Young men, or as they are always called here, "gents," and young ladies also make a number of presents to each other, and even children of tender years hoard up their cents for the purpose of thus expressing their infantine attachments; so that Christmas is always looked forward to by storekeepers as their harvest time. One old gentleman sank into his chair next me at dinner, and confessed that he had been obliged to spend in this way 100 dollars within the last two hours. Every thing here is like old Christmas at home. The market displays as many turkeys, though perhaps not quite so much massive meat as Leadenhall, and everybody is contemplating to-morrow as a day of harmless jollity and round games. On Christmas day the Consul called on me to ask me to come and share a turkey and plum pudding, but I was unfortunately out at the time. I used often to spend half an hour chatting with him at his office, and very entertaining he was. I also became very well acquainted with a Rev. Mr. — who is a very great favourite with his congregation, by whose pew-rents and presents he is well supported. These are the only sources from which an American clergyman derives his income, and where the congregation is pretty "able," they always take care that their minister shall be, if possible, in the same plight. Mr. G— received the other day a present of two bags of coffee, one barrel of sugar, two chests of tea, a few hams, and some loaves of bread; and almost all the ornamental furniture in his house, and books without end have been likewise sent him by anonymous friends. I had a sample of every sort of weather during my stay, and when I left, sleighs were rattling about in every direction, drawn by any number of horses from one to eight, all glittering in scarlet coverings, and jingling with innumerable bells. One of the strangest and oddest habits in the town is that of getting up amateur fire societies. A number of young men, mostly apprentices, will get together, club up their money, form a company, choose a captain, and at a great expence purchase and fit up a fire engine. There are about a dozen of these societies in the city, and on the slightest alarm of fire the members rise to a man, leave their warm beds in the middle of a January night, rush to their engines, which they drag along themselves and are all at the scene of destruction in less than half an hour, and there labour away without fee or reward of any kind. If by the time the fire is got under, they have not had sufficient excitement, they turn their engines on to one another, and the affair often ends in a regular fight, by which bones are not unfrequently broken and the whole town put in an uproar. I was a spectator of one of these odd scenes, and came home with my raiment not over and above dry. I was also present the other day at the opening of a house of refuge for black children, which has been started in consequence of the success which has attended a similar one for the whites. The meeting consisted chiefly of quakers, who are very numerous and do a great deal of good here, and amongst them I espied their brother of steam-packet "devil-take-the-hindmost" notoriety. It was addressed by the principal judge in the neighbourhood, but what a judge! so different to our ideas of those awful individuals with their aged faces marked with so many hard lines and learned wrinkles. He was a young man with weak eyes, turn-down collar, and a large beard, who spoke through his nose for an hour and a half on the state of crime in Philadelphia, which to judge from his account must be a most awful place. The Penitentiary here, from which we took our model for Pentonville, is a very well constructed institution, though not so perfect in its internal arrangements as its copy. The prisoners are allowed to be seen by no one, but some of the cells are exhibited. One of these I particularly noticed, the walls of which were really beautifully painted by a man who had been in prison for five years before he came here. He stayed and decorated his cell here for another five years, and when discharged he commenced stealing again, and in less than two months was condemned to two years in another prison. He decorated the walls of that cell in a most elaborate manner, and is now in Baltimore jail for another theft, and has begun his old pursuit, which, as he has some ten years to stay, will result in some grand masterpiece in the fresco style. This odd talented creature is a German, and extracts his colours from the yarns given out to him for weaving. I left Philadelphia with great regret, and arrived at Baltimore on Wednesday night. It is a large bustling city, with not much to interest a stranger. The country through which the railway passed was covered with snow, which is a sad leveller of scenery. I did not see much worth noticing except the bridges which cross the inlets of the Chesapeake. They have no parapets, and are just broad enough to admit of a single line of rails. The water—or rather ice—was plainly visible through the planks, and the sensation of being rattled at some thirty miles an hour over these risky affairs was very far from being pleasant. Baltimore is the capital of the first slave state, and blacks are to be met at every turn. Many of them are free, but all freedoms "elevation" theories are sadly at fault with respect to them, as they are the most dirty idle rascals to be met with anywhere, and the slaves are twenty times over their superiors in every way. For this their old masters are strictly to blame. They took care that they should be kept ignorant, and should not now wonder that they are brutal. I soon left this place for Washington, where I stayed for ten days, most of which time I spent in the Senate, whose debates used to attract most crowded audiences. During the sittings of Congress in the winter months, Washington is the great place of the States, and the rendezvous not only of noisy statesmen but of speculative mammas and anxious daughters. Washington as a town may be easily described. It was intended by the founder to be the most magnificent city of the union, and was planned in accordance with that idea. A splendid capitol was built, from which avenues were formed branching out towards all points of the compass, though only one of them has been built on to any extent, which stretching west for a mile and a quarter to the President's House, may be said to comprise the principal part of the city. In this street, which is styled Pennsylvania Avenue, lie all the leading hotels and stores, but one side of it only can be said to be respectably built, the other consisting chiefly of straggling markets and meeting houses. Two lines of lime trees run down this avenue, which must make it very beautiful in summer. The Capitol, being

E

the principal building in the town, claims first notice and it certainly is a very splendid affair, built on rather rising ground and commanding rather an extensive view of the Potomac River, which here runs through a very flat but well-wooded country. It is surmounted by an immense dome, which gives light to a large middle hall, from which passages lead to the Senate House on one side and the House of Representatives on the other. This hall has eight pictures round it, five of them commemorative of American valour in the late war, in which disconsolate-looking officers in scarlet are represented as delivering up their swords and persons to exulting officers in blue turned up with buff. The other three refer to earlier periods in the history of the country. They are the baptism of Pocahontas, the meeting of Penn with the Indians, and the embarkation of the Puritans for the country. The last is the best imitation of Maclise I ever saw, and considered the best painting of the eight. The House of the Senate, to which each state sends two members, lies on the north side of the building, and is a large semi-circular room very plainly but very comfortably fitted up with arm-chairs and desks. Plans are sold at the doors, with the names of the senators who occupy each seat, which makes it much more interesting for strangers. Having found my way up into the gallery, which was so crowded that for the first ten minutes I could see nothing but the chandeliers, I was told that the Austrian question as to whether diplomatic relations should be suspended or not, was before the house. General Cass had spoken on it a few days before, and it was thought probable that both Clay and Webster would do so. After about half an hour of pushing and squeezing, I got into a very tolerable place both for seeing and hearing. The chair was filled by the vice-president of the United States, Mr. Phillimore, an English-looking gentleman with a good and rather authoritative voice, which he often had occasion to put in requisition, as honourable senators here are very liable to speak six at a time. On his right, were all the representatives of the southern states, advocates of slavery, and on his left, the northern men, among whom were Clay and Webster, abolitionists. I hear many say that this question will eventually cause a separation of the union. The southern men are mostly distinguished by their long black hair and dark eyes, and looked a different race altogether to their neighbours of the opposition, whose broad massive foreheads and thick eyebrows bespoke a more English origin. I had not been there long before Henry Clay, the lion of Kentucky and the ladies' favourite, got up to oppose the measure, and though upwards of seventy he still retains a most powerful voice. Though he was rather slow in his delivery, he brought out his points with such clearness and force as to well establish the high character I had always heard of him as an orator. He was succeeded by many men of inferior note, most of whom seemed to disdain anything like ornamental language, but came to their meanings at once, and though their grammar was now and then at fault, their pronunciation peculiar and their phrases homely, yet they all seemed sensible and straightforward sort of people. They have a certain Colonel Foote here, the Sibthorpe of the senate, who furnishes an immense deal of amusement to the house. He is much more lengthy in his speeches than his English prototype, and is very fond of concocting elaborately satirical speeches, which he brings down to the house among a great bundle of papers and fires off at intervals amid roars of laughter. As the personalities he perpetually indulges in are never noticed and his arguments are never responded to, a great deal of his labour is lost. There was nothing to hear in the House of Representatives, their precious time having been taken up in balloting for a clerk, whose election occupied three weeks! I did not hear Webster speak in the Senate but was fortunate enough to listen to him defending a case in the Supreme Court, when I was especially struck with his power of condensing matter, and putting the most entangled and difficult case into the clearest shape in the smallest space of time. Hence I became quite interested even in a dull "right of way case" when in his hands. On the 11th of January, I attended the President's levee, which is held at his house, a good substantial building of white stone, every Friday evening, when every body with anything like a respectable appearance makes a point of going. "Old Zack," the name he is generally known by, is the very picture of Sir L— G—, and had I met him in the street I should have stopped and spoken to him at once. The levee was rather a stupid affair, for after having shaken hands with th President, and having been introduced to his daughters, all of whom are married, I was left very much to my own resources. If you know many people you generally spend an hour or so in talking till it is time to withdraw, but if you are a total stranger, the sooner you go the better. After staying at Washington till the 15th, I set off southward. A sharp frost had set in, accompanied with snow, and hence my idea of passing a year without a winter was totally dispelled. That morning was about the coldest I ever remember, and there was a great quantity of ice floating about on the Potomac, but as the sun shone out at intervals very cheerfully, and our steamer was a decidedly fast one, I did not much care. The Potomac river is like the generality of American rivers, broad, slow, and deep, with little of scenic interest on its banks, and what there was the snow had completely effaced. We got on very fast, as the steamer broke with ease through the half-inch ice, sending the fragments aloft and causing great cracks to shoot out on each side nearly as far as the bank. Flocks of canvass-back ducks, unconscious of the savory destiny that awaited them, passed us every now and then, followed by flocks of the black ducks, who seemed to keep at a respectful distance from their more highly-flavoured brethren, while an occasional osprey would dart down on a piece of ice in search of some fancied prize, and then float leisurely down the stream.

CHAPTER VII.

> "I took a dance dat bery night,
> I dance myself clean out of sight;
> De niggs next morning look around,
> Dey saw but a grease spot on de ground."
>
> Ole Dan Tucker.

MOUNT VERNON—AN AMERICANIZED SCOTCHMAN—NEGRO [illegible]—THEIR TREATMENT—[illegible]—[illegible]—CHARLESTONIANA—NEGRO SUPERSTITIONS—TURKEY BUZZARDS—SICK PASSENGERS—NEGRO DANCING—NEGRO AMUSEMENTS—SAVANNAH AND ITS CEMETERY.

In about an hour we passed Mount Vernon, dear to every American, as the home and burial place of General Washington, an unpretending wooden villa surrounded with plantations, and an excellent property. In the summer, crowds of Yankees flock here to pay their tribute of respect to the memory of the patriot, and to eat sandwiches. After a sail of 55 miles, I *joined* "the cars," and arrived in Richmond that evening, passing on my route through a series of tobacco plantations, with a few houses belonging to the planters, near which were little huts occupied by the slaves, whose black happy faces met one at every point. Richmond is the capital of Virginia, and a great tobacco growing place. I stayed here a day on purpose to see this manufacturing process, for which I had a letter of introduction to Mr. S., a Scotchman, who left his country some fifty years since, and has only been back once, about two dozen years ago. He seemed to have become thoroughly Americanised, and I thought he had quite forgotten the land of his birth, but when I mentioned the country about Selkirk and Melrose, where I had walked but a few months before, his heart warmed up, and the old fellow nearly cried. He was born a few miles from Selkirk, on the way to Smailholm Tower. Nothing could exceed his civility; and his son showed me all through the manufactory, in which I saw the slaves looking very smiling, and singing hymns. I am told that negroes, although living in "Old Virginny," never did, and never would, sing such songs as Old Dan Tucker and Lucy Neale, which only originated in the brains of their sham Ethiopian personifiers. The songs they do sing are almost always of a religious turn, something between a nautical anchor-hauling chaunt and the "Old Hundredth." They were engaged in extracting the stalk from the tobacco plant (which looks like a great brown cabbage) and rolling it up and putting it into presses to reduce it to a chewing state, after sprinkling it with liquorice to sweeten it. The negroes seem to be very well fed, and a good man will fetch 800 dollars. Some I saw had been hired at seventy-five dollars a year, and are therefore generally a very good investment. It is quite against a master's interest to use them badly. He has only to feed them well and *take care they do not learn to read and write*, and in most cases they get mutually attached. Some I spoke to said they would not leave that State and go into another for anything, except their master went with them. This town is a great slave mart, and I saw a set of shivering little negroes sitting on show and waiting for a purchaser. They seemed quite callous on the point, and talked and laughed heartily among themselves. There are nevertheless some heart-rending scenes when the slave does not wish to leave his master and is being parted from his wife and children, but masters generally aim at keeping them as much in families as possible. I left Richmond and travelled all day on the railway to Wilmington. Sleeping in an American car, where the seats are all arranged like pews with an aisle down the middle, is a matter of considerable difficulty, for the back of the seat only reaches as far as the middle of the spine, and the great size of the car admits of numberless mothers and babies, which it is impossible by the most subtle artifices to keep all quiet at precisely the same time. On this fatal night, after having been rebuffed and knocked about terribly at every angle, near which I had bestowed my weary head, I at last fell into a sort of a doze, which promised fairly to "eventuate" in a sound sleep. No such good luck was in store for me, as I was shortly disturbed by a something going on at my neck. I did not mind it at first, but at last I became fully alive to my situation, and found that a somebody's baby was trying to thrust a piece of half-sucked sugar candy down between my neck and my shirt, so you may fancy that I got no more sleep that night. When day dawned on myself and my infant persecutors, I found that we were going through a forest, which kind of scenery continued to haunt us the whole day. The railway was flanked by immense pine trees, which started up as straight as a mast. Most of their stems had been tapped near the bottom in order to extract the turpentine, for which the district is famous, and as you rattled by them they presented the appearance of a huge church-yard with the white tombstones appearing and disappearing amongst the trees. Sometimes we passed immense tracts of swamp, over which the pine trees were bending and reflecting their shadows in the dark unwholesome waters beneath. Now and then we stopped at a rude sort of a station, where the land had been a little cleared and some attempts made to plant corn, to further which design, half a dozen rude log huts had been run up, and where the inhabitants more rude still, with their heads quite lost in their immense hats, and their hands quite lost in their pockets, would stand and greet our arrival with a sort of inhuman stare. On we would go again through the same sort of odd scenery, only relieved by some river, over which a slender pile bridge would carry us; sometimes we would pass through groves of white pine or gum trees, on which a beautiful sort of dark moss had grown and hung to it like cobwebs, the bottoms of them being lost in great masses of evergreen called the cacina, which clustered round them in wild profusion. All the forest country was so very unlike anything I had seen before, and presented so many fantastic shapes and shades, that I felt rather sorry when we at last emerged from it, and found ourselves at three o'clock on Thursday at Wilmington. It is a good sized town, situated near a fine river, on which a steamer was in readiness to convey us to Charleston, where, after rounding Cape Fear through waves remarkably smooth for the Atlantic, we duly arrived on the 18th. The town is a very delightful one, but the great charm to me was the weather. I got into the railway on Tuesday morning, with the ground as hard as metal beneath my feet, and the snow three inches thick on every side, and here I sat on Friday morning with a glorious summer sun beaming in at the windows which opened into an airy piazza, and ladies walking with parasols below. The houses here are not so red and glaring as they are generally, but have all the respectability and stamp of age upon them, and the churches have thoroughly English towers and spires. It is situated between two rivers, the Ashley and the Cooper, both of which join the Atlantic at the same place. The coast on each side consists of plantations of Sea Island, Cotton, and a well wooded inviting-looking coast it is, but from the terrible prevalence of miasma it is very fatal to its inhabitants in the summer. I went down with a very pleasant Irishman, who lives at the hotel, to take a look at the docks which extend about a mile facing the Atlantic, whose deep waters come rolling in up to the houses, and quite doing away with any necessity for sluices, dock-gates, and other ponderous and extensive waterworks. There was very little business doing among the cotton brokers and shippers, but as they all stood at the doors of their counting-houses with their hands in their pockets and discoursed quite playfully of bad times, or criticised Mr. So and So's brilliant Madeira, and made up little parties for the coming races, I began to draw conclusions as to how they would conduct themselves in prosperity. I dined to-day with a Mr. H., a bachelor with an handsome income and a liberal table, who when he goes out in the morning orders a four o'clock dinner for half a dozen, and makes up the number from amongst any disengaged friends he may pick up in his counting-house rambles. This practice he has carried out every day for the last fifteen years. The negroes, who here form a great part of the population, are almost all slaves. They are exceedingly good humoured and civil, but have a way of laughing whenever they are spoken to which is quite peculiar to themselves. It is a sort of guttural gurgle, which "Henry Russell" hits off very happily, and whenever you ask them the simplest question they preface their answer with this ebullition of feeling. If you are at some distance from the place you want to enquire your way to, the joke is far too much for them, and you have to wait sometime before you are satisfied on the point. At nine o'clock a drum is beat as a signal for all coloured people, free or slaves, to go home, and any negroes found in the streets after half-past nine are lodged in the guard-house (unless they have a pass from their masters), in which place they are kept till morning, when the master has either to redeem them by paying a dollar, or else leave them to be flogged. In most cases the latter alternative is not resorted to. Mr. H. showed me a mother and five children whom he had bought a few weeks ago; the mother he made a washerwoman of, and the small fry he intended to bring up as servants. The whole five were basking in the sun before their master's steps when I saw them, and they looked remarkably comfortable. One of the little fellows was brought into the dining-room to wait. He was about seven years old, and seemed very proud of his position, and when he has got over his present tendency to carry soup plates on his head, instead of in his hands, and to hum snatches of airs when unemployed, I have no doubt he will prove a most talented Ganymede. In my rides round the outside of the town I observed many large groves of pines and orange trees, the latter of which is a most lovely evergreen, and always preserves a glossy green tint. There was also the live oak, from whose branches hung, in the wildest luxuriance, the moss which pleased me so much in the Carolina forests, and which is supposed to be produced from the dampness of the land about. The wild myrtle and the cacina are also found in great abundance here, and are peopled by robin red breasts, which are as large as thrushes and very delicate eating. The shooting of these birds gives employment and amusement to

J

all the gamins of the town, whose noisy little single barrels, and impudent little faces, are to be heard and seen in every thicket. The offal of the town supports a number of brown Turkey buzzards, which resemble a crow when flying, and a small turkey when walking. They fly close over your head at every turn, and I saw about a dozen of them disputing with some old negresses for the possession of sundry bones which had been left by the tide. They stuck up manfully for their rights, and gave the old ladies no little trouble. I am told that they enjoy protection to the extent of five dollars, the city fine for destroying one of them, and they seem fully alive to their own position in society. On Tuesday, the 22d, I got on board the fastest steamer on the station, to proceed to Savannah, which stopped about four miles from Charleston, to ship a number of wan ladies and feeble looking gentlemen out of a New York steamer, who had passed three dismal days and nights at sea, in the face of an heavy head wind. The latter soon took to smoking and good fellowship, but the former, poor dear creatures, who had been sadly tantalized with the sight of Charleston on a sunny day, either went and shut themselves up forthwith in little cabins, or else lay down on sofas to read "Sidonia the Sorceress," or "Blanche of Brandy-wine," which the steam boat company furnishes in a 25 cent. shape, and under whose small-type influence they soon fall asleep, and forgot the past. After coasting along a flat sandy shore, scantily covered with rushes, we at last entered Savannah River, which was as smooth as a duck pond. Our forecastle was crowded with negroes, who were sprawling about in all directions among bales, pigs, and packages. Some of the young negresses were very sea-sick, and it is absolutely impossible for a goose quill (however ably wielded) to describe the unearthly contortions of face in which they indulged on the occasion. As we sailed up the river they recovered their wonted animation, and after jabbering and grinning at one another in the sun for a considerable time they managed to find a fiddle, and then they were just happy. They have a most wonderful way of adapting their feet to any tune, and whether it be Jeannette or Jeannot, or Yankee Doodle, which their black Paganini might choose to treat them to, Mr. June and Mr. Sambo would on the very first scrape of the bow challenge Miss Louisa and Miss Caroline to stand up and dance the music out. Nothing pleases them better than for any one to stand by and make complimentary remarks on their performance, such as "*Look at that nigger how he dances! That nigger in the black pants* (trowsers)! *He is the regular Jim Crow, he is!*" The nigger so alluded to will instantly throw off his hat and his coat, and begin to exert himself still more, contorting his legs and features most frightfully, and only leaving off when the fiddler gives in exhausted. Their politeness all the time is extreme, and you never hear an improper or uncivil word among them. They have a tendency certainly to get very argumentative, when instead of trying to convince one another by reasoning, they press into their service a number of five or six syllable words, which, though, used quite at random, generally secure a victory to the one whose verbal repertoire is the most extensive. I staid at Savannah with Mr. M. the British Consul, who was excessively kind to me. Turtle, Venison, and Madeira were our daily fare, and many were the good stories I heard from him over the latter. His head nurse proved, after a little conversation, to have been in old times as near a neighbour to me in England, as the Canadian farmer. Savannah can scarcely be called a town; it is in fact nothing more than a succession of straggling villages, with about a dozen village greens, any of them well adapted for may-poles and "groups of happy peasantry." Nearly every row of houses is shaded by a row of olive and orange trees, interspersed with oaks and poplars. None of the streets are paved, so when you walk you invariably sink some two or three inches in sand. The business street of the town is boarded over with pine planks for the convenience of the cotton carts which toil along it, carrying huge bales of cotton to the Press, situated at one end of the wharf, where the bales are pressed into half their original size, and kept till required for shipment. The Savannah river is very narrow and winding near the port, and hence great 900 ton ships appear from a distance to be reposing in the midst of rice fields, their masts and rigging mingling with the pines and other tall trees that fringe the banks. About four miles from Savannah is a piece of forest ground, which has been appropriated for a cemetery, and to see which I had to traverse four miles of the most glorious forest scenery. The road has no fence or walls to protect the woods from intruders, as no one cares about trees being damaged, which grow in such wild profusion. On both sides of it the eye vainly strives to contemplate a tangled incomprehensible mass of foliage, where the vines, the jasmines, and the cacinas are entwined like parasites round the limbs of their stalwart companions, and thorns and hemlock fill up the intervening spaces. Towering above this chaos of vegetation rise giant magnolias, dark cedars, and stout pines as fresh and as green as if they were under a July and not a January sun, and making one look forward to the season when every magnolia is clothed with gorgeous white flowers, when every little creeper contributes its string of blue, scarlet, or yellow berries, and when all the forest is alive with sound, and birds of every hue glance from bough to bough, relieving the drowsy insect hum with their long drawn notes and hasty chirrups. The burial ground to which this beautiful way leads is but newly laid out, and its few white grave-stones are difficult to distinguish amongst the thick shrubs that surround them. It is shaded on both sides by an avenue of live oaks, from whose branches grey moss droops in every form, clothing these forest giants in funereal garb, as they lean in mute mourning over the ashes that moulder beneath.

CHAPTER VIII.

Faneuil Hall was the cradle of the republic, but whar, whar will be found timber enough for its coffin? Scoop all the water from out the Atlantic Ocean, and its bed would not afford a grave for its corpse. And yet America is still in the gristle of boyhood. Europe —what is Europe? She is nowhar—nothing—a circumstance—a cypher. We have faster steam boats, swifter locomotives, larger creeks, bigger plantations, broader lakes, higher mountains, deeper cataracts, louder thunder, forkeder lightning, hansemmer wee-men, more money than England dar have.—*Hesperos.*

THE SAVANNAH CHESTERFIELD—CHURCH DECORATIONS—A NEGRO FUNERAL—AN OXFORD BACKWOODSMAN—THE NEGRO CAR—A RUNAWAY SLAVE—AUGUSTA CULINARY GREASE—A NIGHT CAR —ENGINE FREAKS—A COACH RIDE—AN ADVENTURE—AN EXCITED DRIVER—NIGHT AT OPHELLICA—COTTON FIELDS—ALHABAMA ORATORS.

The society in Savannah is not large, but very agreeable. Mr. M. often took me rides round the Truro, and introduced me to several ladies not in their own drawing rooms, but leaning out of the windows, or over the balconies to enjoy the cool evening air. There is one very amusing young man in the town, who has achieved for himself considerable notoriety by setting up for a Chesterfield, which great authority is seldom out of his mouth. In fact, he seems as necessary to the general conversation, as the state of the weather, or the figures of the cotton crop. His code appears, however, to be founded on the "Two Shilling Guide to Etiquette," and he goes through the most bewildering and excruciating forms, in order to act rigidly up to his principles. The Scotch Church here is the largest in the town, and one of the handsomest places of worship I have yet seen, while the Episcopal Church is a very small one. The people show much more taste in decorating their churches and chapels for Christmas, than in England. It is done in most cases under the superintendance of ladies, and not left to the formal fancies of sexton or clerk. These ladies very often form the choir, and take their places every Sunday in front of the organ like paid singers, and many sweet voices there are amongst them. I lately saw the funeral of a negro, who must have been a person of some note, as he was followed to the grave by nearly a quarter of a mile of his countrymen, and a motley assemblage they were. The hearse was a very shabby low sort of truck, and after it trooped the mourners in very regular double file. The first twelve couples or so preserved the outward trappings of woe very respectably, but after them came such blue trousers, such red waistcoats, such yellow petticoats, and green boots, as to put all idea of a funeral train quite out of one's head. Sunday (on which I saw this procession), is a great day with the blacks in the way of dress, and they exert their most brilliant fancies to make themselves fit to be seen in the afternoon, when they are in the habit of walking out most lovingly, arm in arm with their young ladies. On the 30th of January, I left Mr. M.'s hospitable roof, and took the steamer back to Charleston. We had to go through a chopping provoking sea in crossing the bar at the entrance of Charleston Bay, which soon made me feel that I was only a mortal. I merely staid one night at that place, and then entered a railway to traverse the forests of South Carolina on my way to Augusta. In the carriage I met a gentleman who lived amongst the mountains, in the northern part of the States. He was an Englishman, who was enjoying himself in farming furiously and waging perpetual war against pine and hickory trees, aided and abetted by some half dozen Scotchmen, sturdy civilizing spirits, whom he had brought out with him. He had been at Oxford and was full of anecdotes of the wild time he had spent there, with "Hobhouse," "Yorke," "Beresford," but had now settled down into a perfect "model father," and was heavily laden with tin trumpets, pea-shooters, and a drum or two, for his youngsters in the mountains. Poor man! until the trumpets are bent to the shape of serpents, and two or three holes are drilled through the sides of the drums, what a life he will have to lead! Attached to the train was a Negro Car, something like a huge long barrel on wheels, with small windows in the sides. It was filled with two or three families on the move, comprising negroes of all ages and sizes, who made up for not being allowed to move out on the journey, by making as much noise as they could. The little black boys amused me very much, as some kind master had presented them with enormous new hats, which completely obscured their features, with the exception of their teeth, which in a negro are always to be seen. Indeed if a stranger had looked into that car at night, he would have had great difficulty in detecting anything but teeth, as the cause of all the chatterings, howlings, and laughings, which were perpetually going on. The railway ran through one continual forest, of much the same sort of trees as I have mentioned before, fewer pines perhaps, but more beeches, and birches. On getting out of the car at Augusta, late in the evening, I heard the clank of a chain, and observed a poor shivering negro at my side, with his waist encircled by a strong belt, to which was attached one end of the iron bond, the other end being firmly grasped by a young lad of about 18. I enquired into the case, and the young fellow with the most perfect assurance, rolling a huge piece of tobacco in his mouth, informed me that the negro belonged to a brother of his, and being seized with a desire to see his family in a distant part of the country, had run away, and that he had followed him about 1,000 miles, and was taking him home; adding "*that he was not a bad nigger on the whole, but now and then took strange fancies into his head.*" I asked him if he was not rather frightened to go about with the man, who, though he looked very wretched, was fully six feet high. "*Oh, I guess not,*" said the young slave-tracker, showing me a bowie-knife and a pistol, which he carried like playthings inside his shirt, "*and this here's a considerable thick chain.*" The noise of the fetters sounded strangely, and the poor fellow's face looked very downcast, and no one seemed to observe him. It was a strange sight for an Englishman, and the worst phase of slavery I have seen. Twenty years ago Augusta could only boast of an hotel, a meeting-house, and some few dozen houses; but now a State-house of an imposing appearance, and three streets, each nearly a mile long and twice the breadth of Portland Place, testify to the industry and activity of the inhabitants during that time. I went to see a cotton manufactory, the principal one in the cotton districts, in which, say the sanguine proprietors, lies the germ of a competition, to which Manchester and the north of England, together with Lowell, will eventually succumb. Hitherto they have only made very small progress towards the fulfilment of their wishes, as their spinning and weaving are remarkably crude. I had two or three letters of introduction from some people in Savannah, so that I managed to spend my time pretty comfortably. The hotel was of the worst description, though with an outside show, sufficient to warrant the hopes of an interior, equal to the Euston-square Hotel at least. The bed-rooms were wretched, and the cookery was a complete triumph of grease. That substance floats majestically about the beef-steaks, wholly obscures the sausages, and settles itself hard and thick on the top of every joint. Hot plates and sugar-tongs are unknown, and butter knives considered a superfluity. I have seen the butter itself undergo the most surprising changes in five minutes, wherein it has changed from a bright yellow colour to a sort of variegated one, combining suspicious streaks of black, red, and brown; but the people seemed to like it just as well as ever, for when you looked again it had all disappeared. These unctuous repasts are eaten in long rooms with no carpets or mattings, on table cloths brown from use, and with bone knives and forks of the ancient two-prong shape, and furthermore by the aid of black waiters, whose fingers are too often visible in the very centre of the provisions they bring to you. You may imagine that I was not very sorry to depart for Atalanta, which is about 180 miles distant. We travelled in a great night-car, fitted up with berths or rather sofas, fixed above the regular seats, about a foot and a half below the ceiling, into which the passengers had the privilege of climbing, if they would, or rather, if they could. Short stout men were obliged in this instance to be content with the will, as the deed was impossible. An active person by great saltatory exertion, and putting his feet on the knees and features of some of the sleepers below, *might* perchance arrive at the object of his wishes, and after stupifying himself by repeated blows from the top of the carriage, might get to sleep for a quarter of an hour, when he would have to roll out at the request of the conductor, to assist the engine into its natural track, after a detour, or to start the cars; the engine, from the frosty state of the rails, not being equal to the undertaking. This last service would often take up some time, as the engine could never be prevailed on to pull at the same moment that the passengers pushed. "Now!" would shout the conductor, and for ten seconds the passengers would put their shoulders to the wheel, and exert themselves frightfully, and directly after that, the engine would shriek and puff and strain, but all to no purpose. At last, I began to think it was a sort of practical joke played off upon us by the stoker and conductor, for their own especial amusement, to relieve the tedium of stoking and ticket collecting. These little amusements delayed our arrival in Atalanta till late on Monday, the 4th. Another railway of fifty miles brought us to Griffin, where we had to leave the cars and take to ninety miles of staging in coaches, with leather sides and no glass about them, constructed to carry nine, three on the front and back seats, and three on a cross beam in the middle. This machine I shared with four companions. A most remarkable change in the weather had taken place, and the thermometer which had just before stood at 82° in the shade at Savannah, had got down (the lowest trick it ever served me) to 15° below freezing point, and the consequent state of feet and fingers can be readily imagined. This would not, however, have been so bad if we had been bowling fleetly along a macadamised road at ten miles an hour, with the prospect of an inn fire and no end of broiled ham and coffee

E

about ten o'clock; but to be jolted at the rate of three along a road, or rather track, full of mud holes of unfathomable depth, describing all sorts of perilous angles, as the wheels got in and out; stopping every now and then to allow the driver, axe in hand, to cut out a way for us through some tangled thicket, the regular road having been rendered impassable, and all this by night, is sufficient to make a person think twice before committing himself to the mercy of an American cross-country stage. After passing a miserable night, during which we stopped once at a wretched wooden inn, to be regaled with a feast of (very) fat things, our hopes and spirits began to brighten up, when the morning of Tuesday dawned, and we were allowed to see our danger. During our breakfast at La Grange, our driver, who had not tasted spirits for positively four hours, took that opportunity of indulging copiously in strong drinks, and when we had shut ourselves up in our coach again, we set off, as we thought, with a determination to make up for lost time. At first we were delighted with the improvement in the pace, though we were pitched about like nine pins, but in about five minutes time, when the novelty had slightly worn off, we heard a fearful smash underneath our feet, and came to a sudden stop. The sound of many voices was then heard in our rear, the door was torn open, and a stranger in a soothing voice told us "not to be frightened, as not much damage was done;" asking, at the same time, how many had jumped out? We stared in utter astonishment, and at last were informed that our driver, overpowered by what he had imbibed, had fallen off his box immediately after starting, and that the four fresh horses had dashed on, turned four sharp corners in making the circuit of the town, and had at last been stopped by running against a small tree, about thirty feet high. Ignorance in this case was more than bliss, it was positive safety, for had we known our danger, we might have jumped out and very probably been killed. After travelling all that day, during which my life was again endangered by the driver, who rushed on me, axe in hand, because I objected to being driven any longer by him, we arrived at a little inn in the village of Ophellica, where we had to wait a day for the railway cars. This little place was a fair specimen of a newly-established village, the wood having just been cleared away for the requisite distance on each side and all the huts being of the rudest log material. I passed my night on a sort of couch before the fire, which a negro carefully attended to, as he blacked the shoes. I had been offered half a bed by one of my fellow passengers, but declined the civility. Although I was now and then roused by the fitful dirge of my black friend, who told me he could not rest at night by reason of boots, and left me before it was light to kill a pig, I managed to sleep pretty soundly. After spending an amusing morning in wandering about the woods, the railway took us off to Montgomery, through some large cotton plantations, in which nothing was to be seen but black stubble two feet high, from the tops of which small particles of decayed cotton still hung, and which ploughs, guided by negro women, were busily turning up. Here and there appeared a handsome planter's residence surrounded with wooden slave huts, and nearly in the middle of every estate, stood huge cotton presses with a sort of umbrella top, not unlike so many Robinson Crusoes, or gigantic scare crows. These presses are turned by a couple of mules, and are very expensive. Montgomery, the capital of the state of Alhabama, is fast pushing itself into notice. It is very beautifully situated on the banks of the Alhabama river, and some of the buildings are of solid granite, with very handsome fronts. On the outskirts of the town, is the ruin of the States-house, which was destroyed by fire a few years ago, and has never been rebuilt. As luck would have it, the legislature had hired a room next door to my bedroom in the hotel, and a special meeting to discuss the slavery question (a sorely perplexing one at present) had been convened for this very night. Hence I was not unfrequently disturbed just as I was dropping off, by detached vehement sentences, treating of the star-bespangled banner and the stripes, the American Eagle, and other such like bursts of loyalty.

CHAPTER IX.

"At every door and window,"
Unshaven faces glare;
There's Puke the judge of Tennessee,
And Lynch of Delaware;
And Batter with the long black beard,
Whom Hartford maids know well,
And Wilkinson from Fish Kill Reach,
The pride of New Rochelle;
Elkanah Nutts from Tarry Town,
The gallant gouging boy,
And 'coon faced Bushwack from the hills,
"That frown o'er modern Troy."—Bon Gaultier.

DEPARTURE FROM MONTGOMERY—COTTON-SHIPPING ON THE ALHABAMA RIVER—THE SUBURBS OF NEW ORLEANS—FIRST IMPRESSIONS OF THE TOWN—ITS BUILDINGS AND INHABITANTS—ITS HABITS—DEPARTURE FOR MOBILE BAY—OYSTER FISHING—SAIL FOR CUBA—VIEW OF THE TOWN—SCENE ON LANDING.

I left this place at four o'clock in the afternoon, and reached Mobile after a sail of some 400 miles. The steamer I embarked in was like all others in the southern rivers, but perhaps a trifle more of a caricature in its proportions and build. On an immense barge is erected a warehouse in which the cargo is put, and the engines work. Above this is the saloon, running nearly the whole length of the vessel, one end of which is appropriated to ladies and children, while the sleeping cabins, each containing two berths, are ranged down its sides. The Alhabama river is about one-third the width of the Thames, with low marshy banks covered with wild brushwood and cane-brakes, which form a retreat for thousands of alligators. At present these animals are not visible, being all buried in the sand, but I am told that the summer season brings them out, and that at night the whole river resounds with their croaks. Some parts of the banks are very high and rocky, and the steamer runs close in underneath them, to ship cotton from the many tree-shaded depôts on the top. This shipping cotton is a very pleasant relief to the tedium of the journey, and is managed by the mate of the vessel, who has under his command a gang of negroes and Irishmen, whom he abuses most dreadfully; in fact, I never heard a man swear more in a quarter of an hour than he did. Some of the depôts are furnished with a sort of inclined plane, down which the cotton bales are rolled, which, on their arrival at the bottom, are seized hold of by the labourers armed with hooks, and piled on the vessel. This is a very picturesque process by night, when the innumerable torches of pine wood invest the men, trees, and rocks with a supernatural lurid glare. Owing to these stoppages, it was early on Tuesday morning before I reached New Orleans. The port is connected with the town by a railway, which runs through a most dreary looking marsh, though covered in summer with blue and white lilies and every description of rush and water-plant. After traversing a very French suburb, with little houses, having long windows down to the ground, and long chains stretched across the streets to support lamps, we arrived at the St. Charles Hotel, which is considered the most magnificent one in the States. It is the principal building in the place, and its dome is seen, cathedral-like, at an immense distance, towering above every thing around. Moreover it has a splendid Corinthian front, a good deal larger than the "City" Mansion-House, and is approached by many steps. It was Sunday morning, but the shops were all open, and bands belonging to the various volunteer corps were parading the streets. Idlers of every size and nation—Americans, English, French, Spanish, German, and negroes—were loitering about the streets, or basking in the sun on the steps of hotels, chattering, laughing, and smoking; while crowds of people, the ladies decked out in every variety of summer costume, were on their way to churches, whose bells were heard distinctly above the din of the noisy crowd below. Add to this a beautifully bright sun, and a sky without a cloud, and you may realise my first morning in New Orleans. New Orleans strikes a traveller more than any city in the Union, from its possessing so many foreign features. Like many other cities in this country, it has been built at various times, and in various styles. Some of the houses which were built by the Spaniards, the original founders of the place, still remain mixed up with sundry odd little French cottages, with windows down to the ground, and little balconies stuck on them wherever a piece of bare wall could be found, and the modern stiff wooden American villa. With respect to the St. Charles Hotel, which I before mentioned as one of the principal objects of this crescent city, I must add that there is a statue of some patron saint or States governor (I have not been able to find out which) before the door, which gives it more the appearance of some magnificent temple devoted to the Muses, or some huge States-house, than a place where mortals meet to eat, drink, sleep, or absorb badly printed newspaper articles, brandy cocktails and gin-slings. The people, too, present the most incongruous appearance. Keen-looking Americans from the Arkusan country, far beyond the Mississippi, living on the borders, with cultivation on the one side and buffaloes on the other, and carrying their law in the shape of a savage bowie-knife between their shirts and their trowsers, are to be seen mixed up with their more polished country-men from the south and the east, bearing about them the true Broadway-gents "cut." Negroes of every hue, tightly-strapped thickly moustachoed Frenchmen, sal-low broad-faced Spaniards, whitey-brown looking Ger-mans, and shooting-coated Englishmen, pass and repass you at every turn. The carnival was just over when I arrived, but the only signs of anything like extra-merri-ment were observable among the children, who were here, there, and everywhere, with a mask or a piece of old petticoat on by way of a domino, throwing flour at each other and making some elderly gentleman or scrupulously-dressed young swell very indignant by whitening his coat or getting between his legs. I was in time, nevertheless for a Creole ball, at which I found that, like many other things, the beauty of the Creole women has been sadly exaggerated. You can scarcely conceive a neater and better appointed house in every respect than J——'s. The room I sleep in is a perfect model of a bedroom, and most welcome after the dingy places I have put up with during the last few weeks. The great relaxation for young men of business here is riding out, and hence about three o'clock in the afternoon, the livery stables send forth troops of steeds, which are ridden six miles out and six miles in, along two very bad country roads, after which exciting amusement their riders get dinner and finish the evening at balls, theatres, or operas. The great topic of the place is a Miss ——, whose fortune is stated variously at from £5,000. to £20,000. per annum, and whose accomplishments, prospects, and reported engagements seem to know no end. After a very pleasant stay at this town, I bent my steps towards Mobile, with a view to catching the royal mail steam-ship "Thames" in Mobile Bay, and proceeding by her to Havannah. These steamers excite in the breasts of all those people who wish to visit the West Indies from the States, feelings akin to those entertained by superstitious sailors respecting Phantom Ships and the Flying Dutchman; as their movements are nearly as eccentric and unaccountable. They are advertised to arrive in Mobile Bay on a certain day, and accordingly passengers leave Mobile in small steamers and paddle about the bay till evening, when they return somewhat irate and weary. This generally occurs for three successive days, by which time the patience of the travellers is exhausted and they return to the town, determined to await in future some intelligence of the steamer's arrival before going to meet her. As a general thing, the vessel seems to arrive unobserved, and finding no passengers at the appointed place, turns round and goes on her course, followed by the threats and imprecations of all those left on shore. To obviate these distressing difficulties, I accepted an invitation from the Captain of a vessel lying in the bay, to come and stay with him on board while the arrival of the steamer was in abeyance, and I accordingly left Mobile in company with an Irishman, two Americans, three Frenchmen, and a Jew, to whom the hospitality of the captain had been equally extended. The shipping of the port of Mobile, at least all those vessels engaged in Foreign commerce, are anchored at a considerable distance from the town, and form a very imposing fleet of about sixty strong. A great deal of pleasant familiarity exists between their captains, who pass the main part of their time in paying complimentary visits amongst one another, and drinking complimentary glasses of grog. The only people who feel their sojourn off Mobile to be irksome are the common sailors, who are not allowed to leave their vessels, and are consequently unable to perform that very expensive farce of "Jack Ashore," which generally entails so much expence and loss of character on the actors. Throughout Sunday we waited in anxiety and peered perpetually into the horizon with our telescopes, but all to no purpose and we went to our beds, that is, to our great coats and carpet bags, (there was only one bed in the ship) somewhat dubious as to the existence of a royal mail steamer. Monday morning brought us no fresh assurance on this point, and as no smoke was visible by twelve o'clock, we eventually became reckless and went oyster fishing. These fish are found in great abundance along the southern coasts of America, and form a staple trade of those neighbourhoods, in which they most abound. The entrance of Mobile Bay is especially famed for them, and having put ourselves under the guidance of a Scotch Captain, eminently skilful in finding out the locale of the largest and richest beds, we set forth with a stock of Cayenne pepper, vinegar, and salt, quite bent upon "astonishing the natives." The nearest bed was five miles off, but our guide totally repudiated it, assuring us that he knew of one two miles further, which was infinitely more worthy of our researches. Thither we accordingly went, and were soon up to our knees in water in the middle of the ocean, bringing up the clustering treasures. We had a fine warm sun over our heads, and every species of wild-sea fowl kept piping and screaming above us, or dabbling and diving at a respectful distance. We soon had the boat full, and then with our clothes wet and our fingers scratched, we set to, hammer and knife, and made a glorious meal on our way back to the ship. About four o'clock the next afternoon, we saw the long-looked for steamer gradually looming through the fog; and after many thanks to our entertainer, I got ou board and felt thoroughly rejoiced at being once more under the shade of the blue, white, and red of the union jack. Most of the passengers were Mexicans, good-humoured olive-coloured fellows, who passed the whole of their evenings, and the greater part of their days in playing at Monto, a great gambling game. We had Lady —— and her daughter with us, who had been travelling through Mexico, attended only by one maid. After a splendid passage, we found ourselves one afternoon in sight of Cuba, which possesses one of the finest harbours in the world. On the banks of the inlet, opposite to the town, frowned the Moro, a huge venerable fortress, on whose grey walls the sun was setting brilliantly. The wharfs were lined on all sides with clusters of men in straw hats and white trousers, looking just as if all the Oxford and Cambridge men, equipped for a great boat race, had turned out to greet us. The shapes of the houses were soon visible, and strange shapes they were: some of them were built in long continuous lines, and painted blue, while the cornices and pillars were white. As soon as we came to anchor, the ship was boarded by Spanish officials, and little soldiers in white, with drawn swords, took possession of every gangway, much to the disgust of many of our American passengers. Boats full of jabbering sailors crowded about us, enticing passengers in unknown Spanish, or fearfully broken English, to come on board and be rowed to the town. A report soon got wind that it was the first night of the Huguenots at the Opera House, and when we had got our passports vised, and permits given us to enter the town, our party set off ten strong, eager to get lodgings wherein to deposit our hair brushes, the only luggage that we were allowed to take with us. All the inns were full, but as it was a splendid night, and the bright moon revealed to us a strange sort of town, quite unlike anything in England, except the painted street-scenery of her theatres, we had some most delicious

L

wanderings. One of our greatest pleasures was the difficulty of making ourselves understood. We knew the requisite amount of Spanish to ask questions, but not to understand answers, and every one we met was desperately ignorant of French. My friend the Irishman came out very strong in pantomime, and suited the action to the thought, if not to the word, well enough to signify our wishes regarding beds and lodgings, from which, after giving our hair the requisite turn, we sallied forth to the opera. There, however, we were doomed to partial disappointment, for, after the first act, an apology was made for the rest, in consequence of the illness of the principal singer, and after receiving tickets for the next performance we went away, flattering ourselves that we had been fortunate enough to see the house even, which, owing in a great measure to all the boxes being open, is a more brilliant one than any in England, and considered to rank third to La Scala, at Milan, and San Carlos, at Naples. The ten days I spent here with my hospitable friends were very hot, but the novelty of every thing about me fully made up for the disagremens arising from dust, dirt, and a sun ninety degrees in the shade. It is a place full of interest, beauty, and singularity. Interest, as regards the social condition and habits of the people; beauty, as regards the views from the turreted hills in the neighbourhood; and singularity, as regards every house you enter and every person who passes you. My bed at the W.'s was fitted up in a large anti-drawing-room, ornamented with mirrors, French pictures, and artificial flowers; and I am glad to say that even the mosquitoes respected me, and numerous as were the complaints on every side, I was not bitten once during my stay in the Island. The streets of Havannah are extremely narrow, built so as to screen passers-by from the sun, though what they gain in shade, they lose in dust, jostlings, and almost insupportable odours.

CHAPTER X.

"The sun shines on the Plaza,
But brighter than its beaming,
The lustrous eyes of ladies,
Through mantilla folds are gleaming."—*Taylor.*

STREETS OF HAVANNAH—VOLANTES AND THEIR DRIVERS—IRON-BARRED WINDOWS—GENERAL APPEARANCE OF THE TOWN—EVENING OCCUPATIONS AND AMUSEMENTS—JURISDICTION OF THE GOVERNOR—OF THE GOVERNOR'S WIFE—SABBATH-SPENDING, IN AND OUT OF CHURCH—MONUMENT TO COLUMBUS—NEIGHBOURHOOD OF THE TOWN—NUMBER, EMPLOYMENT, AND PLEASURES OF THE SOLDIERS—HOUSE OF A MERCHANT.

THE most striking object in the streets is the volante or cabriolet, which is drawn by one or two horses, fastened to the end of a long pair of shafts at a distance of two or three yards from the body, which runs along on two immense wheels, and seems to have a very slight connection with its impelling power. The horse is bestrode by a black calesero or postilion, who, though wretchedly cared for about the legs, which are generally decked in the dark livery of nature and armed with spurs, yet preserves a great appearance above, for under a hat of no particular shape is to be seen a white queue of the true old postilion cut, dangling over what has been a laced jacket with odd little tails behind. The continuation of the figure as far as the knees is much in the same fancy style, and the whole ensemble reminds one of a better sort of Guy Fawkes, or a scarecrow which some farmer of taste might stick up in his corn field. With all their strange appendages, however, a volante is only inferior in comfort to a Hansom cab, and if you know sufficient Spanish to direct your calasero, you may see a great deal in two or three hours. He will take you along streets of tawdry yellow houses of one story high, whose windows are protected by long iron bars, at which ladies sit in the evenings to talk and be gazed at; and very often a host of loungers may be seen round one of them containing a bevy of dark-eyed and white-muslined beauties. From the venerable appearance of the town a stranger would naturally look for something in the shape of fine old buildings and churches, or at least some old Murillos or Velasquezs, brought over from the land of their birth by wealthy colonizers, but he is doomed to utter disappointment. Many of the houses are handsome and old looking, but their quaint architecture is disfigured by a still quainter taste, which daubs a massive freestone with blue and yellow paint; and their pictures are of a still lower order. All that I have seen are bad copies or good engravings of modern French masters in private houses, and miserable daubs of virgins and saints in the churches. In street nuisances—to wit, glare, dust, noise, and odours—Havannah stands pre-eminent. To obviate the first of these four evils, the early designers of the town built the streets very narrow, and in so doing have managed to accumulate the other three in all their intensity. The dust is more inquisitive and penetrating, the noise more stunning and unvaried, and the odours more disagreeably piquant than in any place I have ever yet seen. The combination of these four, in addition to the narrowness of the pavement, which would have caused the spilling of much hot blood in the days when to keep the wall side was considered by proud passengers and roystering loungers the test of intellectual as well as physical superiority, makes a traveller, when his curiosity is once satisfied, avoid the town as much as possible in the middle of the day. After he has examined the elegance and variety of the volantes, laughed at the intense confusion of the mule-waggons, whose wheels their drivers seem to make an especial point of locking together for the sake of producing every possible stoppage, and has sympathised with the groups of heavily chained criminals who are employed in mending their own ways and those of the town, overlooked by soldiers with bayonets and task-masters with whips, he has seen every strange sight which the streets can afford by day. At night it is quite different. The mule-drivers have gone to their homes, the criminals to their cells, the dust has subsided, a mild pale-eyed moon has superseded a sun that is not contented without diffusing a temperature of 95 degrees, and the streets are really pleasant. Then fashion stalks abroad, volantes dash about here and there, bearing their duos of beauties, veiled, indeed, but what can one thin layer of gauze avail against the flashings of their dark eyes. Other ladies, also, in all the pride of beauty and gorgeous evening dresses, have come to their iron-barred windows (which have all the appearance of the cages in Wombwell's menagerie, and hold beings as dangerous though not so deadly), and are to be seen engaged in conversation with knots of lounging young cavaliers, returning from the music of the Plaza des Aymer, and on their way for their accustomed ice and cup of coffee at Domenicho's, the great café of the town. A passing peep through these bars gives one a great insight into the domestic economy of families. The father may be seen recumbent and snoring after the burden and heat of the day; the children, dark-eyed and malicious looking, playing on the floor; the gloomy figures of negroes flitting in the back-ground, in connection with coffee-cups and cigars, and the old duenna of the party, wrinkled and strikingly plain, wielding a huge fan with her fat dusky arms, swaying her person in a rocking chair, casting contemptuous glances at the groups in the windows as they whisper their soft nothings, and thinking no doubt of the olden time when she was a window attraction, and such delightful nothings were whispered to her. I was told that, owing to the prevalence of fasting during Lent, I should not see the opera, but this happily proved untrue. It seems that Lent does generally bring with it a cessation from these sort of amusements, but the manager having got Meyerbeer's Huguenots rehearsed and ready, thought it an excellent time to show conjointly his love of music, religion, and full houses, and accordingly applied to the Captain-General or Governor, who is the great potentate of the island, and much more absolute in his authority than even Queen Isabella, to grant him the license requisite for its performance. This gentleman's jurisdiction embraces every person, from the police force to the opera corps. In opera affairs he is really of the greatest service to the public. If, for instance, a sullen basso, a captious tenor, or a spoilt prima donna gets up an indisposition, a sore throat, &c. at five minutes notice, to suit some particular whim, or under the influence of the same feelings sings out of tune, though he or she be backed by the certificates of all the Brodies or Lococks of Cuba, nothing can prevent this prompt benefactor from arresting the offender, and signing an order for a week's meditation in jail. However, though he be the ruling man in the place, he is by no means the ruling power, as report will have it that he is quite subject to his wife, who is a very serious woman, and a close observer of the most minute requirements of her creed. As a matter of course she sets her face against the opera, and, of course, so did her lord. "But suppose," urged the persevering manager, "that we call it '*El triompho del fe*' (the triumph of faith)!" "Ah! that's a good idea," said the lady; ditto, said her husband. This idea seemed to effect a happy combination of amusement and religion. "But," urged the lady, "the leading singer has to sing '*Mort al Papa*' (death to the Pope); that will never do!" "But we can alter that," said the manager, "and he shall sing '*Vive al Papa*' (long live the Pope)!" This alteration made no matter, it did not interfere with the score, and the opera, with numerous excisions was duly performed, to the intense delight of both audience and manager. People went to see it last Sunday after they had spent the morning at mass, the afternoon at a bull fight, and when they were looking forward to a masked ball as a grand finale to their Sabbath revelry. The principal church here has a very handsome monument, and prides itself on possessing the ashes of the great Christopher Columbus, though another in Madrid, and a third in Barcelona, puts in a strong claim for the honour. The ashes of this illustrious navigator seem to have been as freely circulated as were those of John Wickliffe. In the case of the latter "arch heretick," (if I can summon up my Blunt's Reformation), the officers of the

Council of Constance "cast them into the Swift, which bore them to the Avon, that to the Severn, the Severn to the sea, to be dispersed unto all lands, which things are an allegory." There is little worthy of general notice in the churches, as their ornaments and architecture are tawdry and painted to a degree. Religion seems a very secondary concern, and the services are performed to laughing ladies and ogling gentlemen, by priests who regularly attend the aforesaid bull fight, the opera, and masked ball, as soon as the morning's mass is disposed of. The neighbourhood of the town as seen from a fortified hill near the sea, is very fine. On one side is the sea, more intensely blue than I ever saw it, and encircled by a delicate border of creamy spray, which the heavy rolling swell casts up on the rocky coast which is stretched out on each side. Looking in the opposite direction one may see a country undulating and varied, its rounded eminences crowned with majestic groups of palm and cocoa-trees, and dotted by the white wooden villas of those few residents who have had the moral courage to fly from the attractions and dust of the town. Just below is the gaudy town, above which the Cathedral, the Opera de Tacon (a very splendid building), and an immense palace, which is owned by a rich merchant, and is nearly as large as Buckingham Palace, lower conspicuous. A little to the right lies the Cerro, the Kensington of Havannah, approached by the Passeo, or "Rotten Row" of the place, which extends for about a mile, and is skirted by cocoa trees and palms with a delicate fringe of rose trees. The principal merchants live out in this direction, and may be seen bowling along home in their handsome volantes, as soon as their counting houses are closed. On one side of it is a hill of some height, crowned with a formidable fortress, and on the opposite sides of the bay are three or four other hills equally well garrisoned with troops of insignificant little soldiers, white in every part but their faces, which are rendered very tawny by marching and sentinel duty under a Cuban sun. Havannah contains about 18,000 of these soldiers, and the island something like 50,000, so fearful are its Spanish possessors of their enterprising acquisitive neighbours from the American continent, who have already threatened their town with an invasion, got up, in defiance of international law, by private speculation. The yellow stone walls of the town are guarded by nearly as many of these soldiers as a besieged city. Those of them who are not thus employed seem to pass their time in promenading the streets with a most relentless drum, arousing every one at six in the morning, and in disturbing people's reflections at night by hailing them in most unintelligible Spanish. If the questioned one does not answer properly and promptly "Espanhar" (Spaniard) to the first hail, and "Paisano" (citizen) to the second, he either gets a shot sent after him, or a body of these little white heroes will spring on him and carry him off in triumph to the guard-house. The house I stayed in might well be called the abode of a "merchant-prince," at least of a prince in a hot country. Like all other dwellings in the place it had only one entrance, and that partially blocked up by volantes, so that clerks and customers, ladies and negroes, horses and carriages, all entered by one way, and that through the coach-house. In the midst was an enormous court-yard, in which, piled up in the most sumptuous confusion, were to be seen most of the manufactured goods of Europe. Really everything seemed to be there, from the delicate lace of Valenciennes and the silk of Lyons, down to the ginghams of Manchester, the woollens of Bradford, and the sober sacking of Dundee. At the further end of the court-yard was the stable, where half a dozen horses, with their tails carefully plaited and fastened to their sides, were enjoying themselves in peace and plenty. On each side of the court-yard were two tiers of galleries, into which opened the bedrooms of masters and men. At the back of the first story were ranged spacious counting-houses, peopled with clerks, who smoked the rarest cigars and cigarettes over their ledgers and letters. Everybody smokes here, from the grandee lounging in his evening ease, to the black washerwoman over her steaming tub. In a great broad passage behind the counting-house, through which circulated every available breath of air, was placed the dinner-table, on which, at ten o'clock, breakfasts, commencing with iced claret, and at six o'clock, dinners, winding up with coffee, were served up to master, guests, and underlings. Over the front entrance was a beautiful drawing-room, sixty feet by thirty, with a marble floor, and ornamented with huge vases of artificial flowers, in one corner of which stood an Erard's piano-forte, on which one of the partners, a German, played with most wonderful execution.

CHAPTER XI.

"They buried Silas Fixings in the hollow where he fell,
And gum trees wave above his grave,—that tree he loved so well;
And the 'coons sit chattering o'er him, when the nights are long and damp,
But he sleeps well in that lonely dell, the *Dreary Possum Swamp*."
THE BOOK OF BALLADS.

DEPARTURE FROM CUBA—A SUNSET IN THE MEXICAN GULF—INUNDATIONS ON THE MISSISSIPPI—THE SETTLERS—STEAM BOAT PASSENGERS—THE OHIO RIVER—ST. LOUIS—IMAGINARY LOG BOOK—A DISASTER—OFF IN EARNEST—SKETCH OF THE VOYAGERS—SEAFARING TROUBLES.

MY time here at last drew to a close, and I crossed the harbour on the night of March the 8th, not without some regrets at leaving pleasant Cuba, and many wishes that I could have stayed in it a week longer; and sailed out of the bay a little before sunrise when all the town was beginning to glitter in the grey twilight, and the massive Moro to look as cheerful as it could under the peculiar circumstances of its construction. This letter is written on board the Falcon, which is bearing me back again to New Orleans. I am in the enjoyment of lovely weather, and in the company of some very dreary people bound to California, who seem to have quite mislaid all their natural smartness of tongue under the influence of their golden visions. Most of my time was spent in lounging under an awning on deck, reading a book and dozing by turns. Yesterday evening was rather an exception to this monotonous life. The afternoon of a very close day had brightened up, and the sun was beginning to set in all its glory over the Mexican Gulf. It was moreover a Sunday, a fact that was very difficult to realize as the passengers seemed to have quite forgotten its existence, and perfumed the quarter-deck with their tobacco or played furiously at Monto on the forecastle. Amid all the din, I slipped away to a snug little place near the stern, and found many rare subjects for contemplation. I never witnessed a more enchanting sunset, and as the sun kept sinking and sinking beneath the distant wave boundary, it burnished up the sails of innumerable little nautili, which came gliding right up to the ship and then disappeared. I could see their little pearly bodies gradually fading into the depths below. Some of them were of a most gorgeous purple hue, and as a stray breeze wafted them past, they looked like little beings from another world. Who can wonder that our superstitious ancestors found numberless water deities to guide their fragile craft, and that the whole race of fairies, nymphs, mermaids, and water sprites, were implicitly believed in and celebrated in song for ages, when there were such materials as these, wherewith to "build the lofty rhyme;" for who but Queen Mab could have tenanted such mansions and hid in them her team of atomies, and her whip of cricket-bone, with its lash of film? The flying fish too were in a high state of rejoicing, never rising till the huge black bow of the vessel was right upon them, and then skimming over the ripples for a few yards, as if they did it more for pleasure than for fear, conscious of their own freedom and careless of our power to harm them. But I am growing sentimental, so I will only add that my pleasant musings anent these treasures of the deep, and old scenes and faces far away, was suddenly disturbed by a touch on the shoulder accompanied by a gruff Hibernian ejaculation of "Supper's ready!" During the whole of the 11th, it was very rough, and in order to subdue my rising emotions, I was obliged to spend my time entirely on deck, and great was my delight when I found myself on the following day sailing up the broad and muddy Mississippi, and hoping to be at New Orleans in two or three hours. I only stayed there a day, and then embarked upon a Mississippi steamer for St. Louis, *alias* the Queen of the West. The first 1000 miles of the voyage were singularly uninteresting. There had been a great overflow, and most of the trees and houses on the banks, were two or three feet deep in water; and if the latter had not been raised some distance from the ground, the rooms would have been inundated. It was not an uncommon thing to see a man with a cart and oxen, and a few ragged children, standing on a sort of island divided from the house and the other parts of the premises by two or three feet depth of water; his field flooded, his fences broken down, and a few ravenous Turkey buzzards clustering round the dead body of an ox or sheep, which had died from exposure to the wet and cold. Notwithstanding these little troubles, I was told that the people contrive to live and make money. Their principal occupation on first settling is cutting wood for the steamers, that ply up and down the river, which is sold at from one dollar and a half to two dollars per cord, (a bundle six feet long, four feet high, and four feet broad) and a man by hard labour may cut down two cords a day. The wood when cut is piled up in rude flat bottomed barges, which are pushed out to meet the steamers. After a man has made a little money in this way, he begins to cultivate the land he has cleared, and raises a crop of wheat or barley. Some of the settlers have arrived at great neatness in the structure of their little cottages, and the fencing in their gardens, but they can never be secure from inundations, which in one night may sweep away the labour of years. In the summer season, too, they are certain to be attacked by fever and ague, and not a single person that I saw, had a really healthy look. In the first 500 miles, I observed many sugar plantations, with a whole village of negro houses attached to each, as well as respectable two storied houses, with plantation and offices. These are inhabited by the plantation owners, in the winter season, but at the approach of the hot weather, they are all deserted, for no one who has the means of spending a summer in the north or in Europe, would like to tempt the miasma arising from the river mud. The feathered tribe are very happy notwithstanding, and the flocks of wild ducks, geese, pelicans, herons, cranes, snipes, king-fishers, and Turkey-buzzards, which we disturbed in our course, furnished us with much cause for amusement and contemplation. Our fellow-travellers mostly consisted of the lower class of western men, called the "Hoosiers," who employed the greatest part of their time in playing at cards and lounging about the decks, or sitting smoking with their feet elevated some distance above their heads. In this style they would discuss rifle matches, and read twenty-five cent. novels, till the bell rang for dinner, at the first twinkle of which the whole crowd of them would be in motion, and after gorging themselves for ten minutes (the regular American allowance for dinner), would relapse into their former argumentative or tranquil state until supper, and so on, day after day. After a week's sailing, we arrived at Cairo, the mouth of the Ohio. Cairo was originally intended for a large thriving town, and the situation is well adapted to carry out that idea. It is at the mouth of the two mighty rivers, but a great inundation came and confounded the plans of both architect and surveyors, and now it only presents the appearance of a few floating houses, (half of them are, in reality, nothing more or less than dismantled steam-boats,) entirely surrounded by water. The 175 miles from this place up to St. Louis, present a totally different scene. The river was rather low and the banks consisted of picturesque rocky "bluffs," which rose in some places to the height of three hundred feet, and were covered with tall gaunt looking plane trees, with a thick hazle and cotton-tree undergrowth. At length, after having to lay up two whole nights to avoid running on "snags," (timber rafts,) we arrived at St. Louis, which is a large prosperous town containing rather more than one hundred thousand inhabitants. It is the great depôt of the "Far West," and into it are brought all the furs and other articles produced by the settlers in the prairies, and the Indians. Not the least interesting productions from these parts are the people themselves, who are to be met with in great numbers, in all sorts of costumes, half civilized and half savage. The trade of the town is entirely carried on by steamers, which navigate the river to New Orleans, and go up the Ohio to Louisville and other towns which lie in an easterly direction. The artificial wharf here is a very striking work of art. From St. Louis I sailed down the Mississippi again to the mouth of the Ohio, and then three hundred miles up that river to Louisville. The banks of the Ohio are much more interesting and some of the rocky "bluffs" are picturesque to a degree. We soon got quite out of the region of swamps and overflows, and pretty little manufacturing towns, with some very handsome factories and iron-foundries, standing prominently out, often met our eyes. I staid at Louisville a day, and then started for Cincinnati. Besides its oil-cake manufactories, Cincinnati is the slaughter-house of America, as about 120,000 hogs are killed there annually and packed and sent off to all parts of the country. It is a very handsome town, flanked on one side by an enormous rock, along which are manufactories of every sort—iron, cotton, flax, flour, and steam-engine. Landusky, on Lake Erie, was my point from thence, and I crossed that lake by steam-boat to Buffalo, where I staid a very few hours, and then crossed the Lake Seneca to Geneva, where I joined the railway, which traverses a very wild rocky country on the banks of the Delaware river. The snow was just breaking up on the hills, and torrents of every size were pouring over the cliffs, and sometimes coming on to the tops of the carriages, if they happened to be passing the foot of a very steep eminence. I arrived at New York the next morning, and put up at my old hotel, where I found a number of well-known faces. Unfortunately all my letters had been sent to Mobile, and I instantly telegraphed for them, in the faint hope that they may arrive before I embark on the good ship ——— for a forty days sail to Rio Janeiro. I write this in lat. 4.50, by lon. 36.50, having been on "the sad sea waves" for full thirty days, and having contrived to get pretty pleasantly through the hot tropical days and the long still nights, by the aid of rat-catching, shark-fishing, Macaulay and the Portuguese Grammar, &c. To begin with the first day of sailing, and to give you the regular daily accounts of my voyage hitherto, is a thing I shrink from, for I should be sorry to inflict on any one the trouble of reading 30 or 40 entries like the following :—" April 20, *First up this morning with the exception of the man at the wheel, who had been up all night—Found the sea very high, looking blue in some places and white in others—Saw two ribs of sea weed (speluncarius maximus)—The mate, who was dressed in a tarpaulin hat and wide trowsers, said they came from the Bahama Banks—Steward announced breakfast—Salt cod and potatoes—Felt sick, partly from the cod, partly from the motion of the ship—Went on deck—Thought I saw a shark, but didn't—Saw a sail beating to windward, thought it was a Dutchman, but it wasn't—Captain tried to speak it, but couldn't—Dinner came, ate some apple duff (a sea name for apple pudding)—After dinner the men caught a baracouta, a fish which they told me laid three eggs every year and sat on them for a month—The wind got up, hoped it would go down, but it wouldn't—Tried to sleep, but couldn't—Thought I had a flask of brandy with me, but hadn't—Turned in at* 10 *o'clock—Hope to be up first to-morrow, &c.*" Thus could I fill countless pages with perfectly true and uninteresting details, but in the perusal of which you would find small amusement and soon grow mortally weary—and no wonder. I must therefore huddle up into a two sheet space, my experiences of five weeks in the little wood and canvass world, of which I am now an important member. On the 13th of April, 1850, exactly six months after my first leaving England, having taken an affectionate leave of all my New York friends, I committed myself and my fortunes (i. e. two portmanteaus, two carpet bags, and a hat box) to the barque, a Baltimore clipper of 350 tons burden. A tug steamer took us out of the harbour, perhaps the finest in the world, towed us about four mile into the bay, and left us in a perfect calm, lying between Staten Island and Long Island. We soon had the vessel decked out with canvass, and looked expectantly to two or three black clouds to the westward, which seemed to betoken wind. In five minutes from that time, the ship was on her beam ends, a squall sudden and imperceptible as those of the Archipelago (of which Titmarsh sings so pleasantly in his trip to Cairo), had come up the bay, and struck her. In two minutes more, the foretop gallant-sail split with a voice of thunder, and flapped about in most pitiable shreds—the sails were strained to their utmost tension; and in about five minutes after that, we were tearing back towards the place from whence we came, with the speed of a racehorse—and a quarter of an hour saw us safely moored again off the wharf, with our ensign torn to shreds, a melancholy wreck of stars and stripes, and our captain in anything but a good humour. As the two above-mentioned articles had to be replaced, a boat was sent ashore, and I with it, happy in the contemplation of one more quiet dinner and bed at the hotel before I again essayed a voyage, to which I had had such an unpleasant prologue. The next morning, according to appointment, I met the captain on the wharf, and after a long pull over a heavy surf, we shipped our sail, our ensign, and ourselves, on board the bark, and with a spanking westerly wind rattled out of the bay at a great pace, to the intense delight of our noble captain, who was making his first voyage in that capacity. "*She's a bird—she's a bird—she don't want no steam, she don't,*" were the ejaculations of that enraptured official, as we passed quickly along the Sound. Great Liverpool packets toiled after us in vain, and even steamers impeded by the heavy shore surf, could not catch our Baltimore clipper. Staten Island on the one side, and the New Jersey shore on the other, shone forth in all their morning magnificence, thickly covered with the little white retreats, which form the evening solace of many New York merchants and store-keepers. All these made now a really *moving* panorama, and we could catch now and then the sound of the early chapel bell, the last we should hear for many days, collecting and reminding its hearers of the services and duties of the Sabbath. After about two hours hard sailing, we hove to, and discharged our pilot, who with great intrepidity resigned himself to a very nutshell of a boat, in which he was tossed cruelly before he reached his trim built clean looking craft, which was waiting for him at a distance of about 200 yards. On then we went again, and by 10 o'clock, land had become a thing of conjecture. As a vessel of 300 and odd tons could not be expected to furnish much social accommodation, our passengers and cabin capabilities were limited. A yellow little Frenchman, about 45 years of age, with wonderfully sparkling eyes, and a most pleasing expression, was my first acquaintance. I saw him at first in rather a delicate situation, for from out of two bulky trunks, he was producing several massive instruments like telescopes which the captain who was with him, was handling and eyeing suspiciously, for they were being offered as collateral security for the payment of passage money, on the ship's arrival at her destination, and the captain, shrewd though he was, was not a little puzzled. In this transaction, which at last was satisfactorily settled, he was assisted by his companion and fellow passenger, another Frenchman, but cast in a different mould. He was a stalwart man, also of about 45, with a bald head, jet black moustache and beard, and a saturnine look with him; he spoke English very fairly, but had a dreadfully unpronounceable name, which the captain without any authority or analogy, shortened immediately into "*Doctor*," which appellation he now bears with great complacency. My third and last companion is a Mr. B——, a well informed, rather wild, and very argumentative Yankee, from the banks of the Hudson. His principal weakness is a species of idolatry for his great countryman Henry Clay, whom he contemplates as towering high above his fellows, either in his own or any other country, and indeed his retrospection as regards that great man, is the only inferior position in which he is ever disposed to regard himself. Our dinner party on the first day was a very exciting affair, we were obliged to hold on to our plates with one hand, while we fed ourselves knife, fork, or finger-fashion with the other, and the number of misdirected potatoes and stray waifs of gravy, were piteous to behold. The wind towards evening increased into a gale, but with one melancholy exception (myself), everybody was exempt from sea sickness, and whilst the Doctor enveloped himself in the folds of a large cloak, and darkly contemplated the storm from a corner and Mr. B—— was "keeping himself on his sea legs," as he called it, by repeated and lengthened applications to two demijohns of brandy ; I retired a deadful object to my berth and soon relapsed into a state of dogged insouciance. This was broken into now and then by strains of music, and looking across the cabin I could descry the little Frenchman, guitar in hand, fenced into an immoveable position by his two trunks and a great chair, and thence amongst the "roar and the rattle," was he fingering forth portions of the complaints of Norma, the address to Susannah (the Negress), and the dirge of Old Uncle Ned, in a way very soothing to a sick ear, and for which I silently but fervently blessed him.

CHAPTER XII.

"All day the wind blows low with mellower tone:
Thro' every hollow cave and alley lone,
Round and round the spicy downs the yellow Lotos dust is blown.
We have had enough of action and of motion we,
Rolled to starboard, rolled to larboard, when the surge was seething
free,
When the wallowing monster spouted his foam fountains in the sea.
Let us swear an oath, and keep it with an equal mind,
In the hollow Lotos-land to live and *lie reclined*
On the hills like gods together, careless of mankind."

THE LOTOS EATERS.

TROUBLES OF THE STEWARD—SUNSETS—HAILING SHIPS—THE CAPTAIN AND HIS MATES—RATS—MARINE SPORTING—AMATEUR ASTRONOMY—FIRST SIGHT OF LAND—A SUNRISE AT THE BRAZILS—A LAND SMELL—A CHANGE OF DRESS—RECEPTION IN PORT.

UP to Tuesday night, the gale continued with the same force, but that night, it dreadfully increased. Our mainsail gave way with a thundering noise, and even the captain, backward as mariners are to own anything like fear, confessed it was a regular "*tunnay-do*," and "*he had never seen it blow harder.*" The view from deck was frightfully appalling; perhaps not quite so startling a water work as Niagara from Table Rock, but more drearily magnificent. In the former, grand though it is, you remember you have nothing to do with it but admire; that you can look at it till you are giddy or tired, and then go; but from the latter there is no retreat. You are in the very heart of it, and any one of the enormous liquid mountains up which you seem always climbing, but never surmounting, may turn out of its course, and in one second crush you hopelessly and irretrievably. Such is the time to make one thoroughly feel one's own littleness, and marvel at the intrepidity of mortals in trusting themselves and theirs to the strength of a few inches of wood to divide them from death, in the middle of its most powerful agents, and to find clearer proof, if such were needed, of the combined might and mercy of an Almighty Power. The most burdened man, for the first three or four days, was the steward, a half-caste, who was always complaining of his legs and arms; and with reason, poor man, for his existence during that period was one unceasing conflict against angles, a life composed of ups and downs. His prescribed duties were in themselves considerable: he had three breakfasts to cook, and wait at; sundry fowls to kill, anatomise, and prepare for three separate dinners; three teas to serve; all the knives, plates, and forks to clean; five beds to make, and all the sweeping to do; but in addition to these duties, he had to keep himself from falling, to make frantic rushes every now and then to prevent piles of crockery from tumbling down; to stop the dog, an animal brought on board to kill rats, from devouring the dinner before it was half cooked; and finally to be washed at least once in every hour from caboose to cabin, in the conveyance of his savoury treasures. I remember complimenting him, on the third day, on his cookery. "*Wait,*" said he, "*till we have fine weather, and then I'll show you what I can do.*" Hardly had the unfortunate man uttered these words, when an enormous wave burst suddenly upon him, and carried him from one side of the vessel to the other, rolling him completely over. For some time we saw him struggling in the distance with a pile of dirty plates which he happened to have about him; but ere long he returned, thoroughly wet through, without a plate broken, and, with a passing complaint on his legs, retired into his caboose, and immediately commenced making pastry. Truly, he was a wonderful man! The weather did not become pleasant till the Monday week succeeding our departure; we had, however, made a very fast though rough run, and the mild atmosphere, the glorious moonlight nights, and the sunsets were delightful—such sunsets—such tints—such colouring in them; it required but a slight stretch of fancy to discover islands upon islands, lakes upon lakes, formed by the shapes of the clouds—some dark, lowering, and surrounded with masses of liquid fire; others seeming as though they had been steeped in other sunsets far away from our earth, from our sun, and from our ken. To eyes which all the day had been limited to an horizon six miles off, on every side, these heavenly evening landscapes were a great relief, and the contemplation of them, as I lay stretched on my back on the quarter deck, has been one of my greatest pleasures during the voyage. On that particular Monday, the first day of fine weather, we inspected all our live stock, and six pigs, six geese, and thirty cocks and hens, were soon rambling about the deck in high feather, and with delighted grunts. Amongst the thirty there was of course a good deal of cooped-up feeling to show, and we had no less than six distinct fights in the first quarter of an hour. The conqueror by that time was proclaimed, or rather proclaimed himself from the top of the long boat, a position he maintained for fully a fortnight, when he was called upon by the executioner, alias the steward, to figure in a fricassee, and managed, with the assistance of a little curry, to make himself very pleasant there. Up to this time we have passed four or five ships: the first an Englishman, the second a Dutchman, full of emigrants, bound to New Orleans. How they did flock in clusters to the side to look at us as we passed! They had been two months at sea, and I can fancy their pleasure at contemplating something which would break the dulness of the never-ending horizon. A Swede was our next meeting: we lay becalmed for a day within a mile of him, but had no communication, for the captain said "*What's the good of talking to a feller as don't understand English.*" Our next rencontre was at night. A dim outline of a ship was descried; we showed a light, and it was answered; and presently a tall dark monster loomed out of the distance, and as he bore down upon us seemed as if he would overwhelm us in his majesty. He fell off as he approached, and as he passed under our stern a hoarse summons came out of him, breaking over the water in terrible gruffness—"*Washipsatt?*" "The —— ——, thirty-one days from New York to Rio," says our captain, who seemed to have understood that awful question. "*Washipesay?*" Our captain repeated his former answer, and then asked who *they* were? and it was then that "*Nitidstayshippoke bowdookalyforny*" (United States ship, Polk, bound to California) came in all its mighty indistinctness. We then got out of him that he was thirty-four days out, and had been becalmed eighteen days; and after a few mysterious communications about longitude, we parted, raced with him for two days, and then lost sight of him. The captain hopes to beat him into Rio, where he is going to stop. Our captain, L—— by name, is a true specimen of a long-headed cute Yankee. He seems to have had little regular education in his youth, as he entered the service of the sea as a cabin-boy, and has worked himself up through every grade to his present situation. He has been to all quarters of the globe except the far East, and in every place has been especially observant of men and manners. Dickens, Thackeray, James, and Mrs. Gore are his favourite authors; he dotes on the Life of Lord Byron, and often walks the deck muttering to himself, "*All earthly things shall melt in gloom,*" which he thinks the finest poem extant; or humming selections from "Somnambula." He constantly asks me questions about Queen Victoria, whose mortality he evidently doubts, and is not quite certain whether she eats, drinks, and sleeps like other people. He once asked me if dukes were good enough people to dine with her, and has treasured up little facts about her coronation and marriage, which I had quite forgotten or never heard. It is his delight to tell of contests between Englishmen and Americans, and whether it be in feats of dexterity, of physical strength, or 'cuteness, I have always the mortification of hearing, that the latter were decidedly victorious. He calls our Gallic companions "*Mounseers,*" and both himself and Mr. B— thoroughly despise them; a feeling which is returned with compound interest by "The Doctor." On what may be called the threshold of our society (for they sleep at the entrance of the cabin), are the two mates, the greatest character of which is a Scotchman, who to judge from his jaundiced tone whenever he speaks of the Scotch lasses, left his native land in consequence of a love-reverse, and enlisted under the American flag. He speaks in raptures of the way in which American sailors are fed, and from his account, Scotch captains almost starve their crews. Rio is not one of his favorite ports, for it seems that when he was there last, he fell in with some companions, North Britons, and that after a little jollification in honour of the land of their births, they behaved themselves rather noisily in the streets, and our hero was confined in the lock-up for two days, with nothing to eat: this last grievance made such a deep impression on him, that he said he would never set foot on shore again. We have hooked two or three sharks, but have not had the good fortune to secure one yet, our lines and hooks giving up in the moment of victory. The rats have been our chief enemies: when we are all in bed they come out and make a night of it, and by the light of the lamp we can see them disporting themselves on the cabin floor—when called to they pay no attention but turn coolly round and chatter at you in your berth, and it is only the immediate presence of a shoe or the end of a broomstick that will at all intimidate them. We set circular traps hung round with nooses, by which means we have caught about fifty, and handed them over to the jaws of our dog, by whom they are soon finished. We have caught several of Mother Carey's chickens by means of pieces of pork attached to strings—these birds come in clusters over the pork and get entangled in the string,—they are the smallest of all web-footed birds, and possess the sharpest black eyes in the world.—Saturday, 25. A succession of calms and contrary winds have delayed us very much,—we came in sight to-day of three rocks, the first land we have seen, called the "Abrothas," about four hundred and twenty miles from Rio, so that if we have anything like good luck we ought to be at our journey's end by Tuesday. Many were the lingering expectations with which we paced the deck on the afternoon of the 29th of May. We had a light wind all day, and as we looked over the ship's side and found that our movement was only just perceptible, we almost gave up any hopes of seeing the Brazils before the next day. At last the outline of what had seemed for some time nothing more than a faint blue cloud on the horizon, began to assume something like consistency, and the Captain pronounced it to be the long-wished for Cape Trio. To this we all joyfully assented, except the Doctor who held on strenuously for some other Cape, as he brought his double-barrelled lorgnette to bear on it. This was only one of many struggles of opinion that had been carried on between these two. Their disagreements had been perpetual during the voyage. We caught a fish one day, which the Captain forthwith pronounced to be a baracouta, and good to eat,—while the Doctor said it was something else and poisonous. However, little of it remained after dinner but bones, and I believe we are all now in sound health. The Doctor one day in direct defiance of the popular superstition, amused himself by shooting at Mother Carey's chickens with an old horse pistol, which greatly incensed the Captain, deeply tinged as he was with the belief that they are the dwellings of the spirits of departed sailors, and he would not have been easily pacified, had not the recoil of one of the discharges severely blackened the intrepid sportsman's eye. About distances, too, they could not hit it at all. The Doctor had a sort of mental scale of latitude and longitude, deduced from the stars and his lorgnette, with which he would delude himself and his little friend. The latter would come skipping up to me to tell me the the result of his countryman's investigations. "*Bravo*" he would say, only "*deux degrees de longitude von hundred twenty miles,*" while the Captain, whose observations had just put it at eight degrees, would look on grimly smiling. However, the Doctor at last gave in about Cape Trio, and as the wind rose with the moon at about ten o'clock, we passed within six miles of it, and began to be affected with that nervous tendency to pack up, experienced by all travellers who are within a day of their journey's end. At five o'clock next morning, we were all up looking forward to what with me was to be the greatest scenic treat I had ever yet experienced. At that hour all was grey and hazy, and the shape of many mountains was dimly visible on the right as we coasted gently past them at a distance of some five miles. Presently the east began to give some signs of activity and to throw out a faint red bloom, which tinged with the most delicate blush, the little fleecy scirri lying motionless on the verge of the horizon. Gradually the bloom grew deeper and deeper, and the little scirri disappeared in the increasing glory. The top of the great red disk revealed itself, at first compressed and angry-looking, but soon darting out gleams of yellow which acquired brilliancy and power every moment, till the eye became dazzled and the whole face of the deep was in one rich glow. Then on looking behind at the land, what a view awaited us! The curtain had risen on a fairy prospect; the touch of twenty minutes had changed the scene—a new country had burst into life! What before had seemed grey and hazy, was now glowing in every colour—mountains rose out of mountains, those near the coast grotesque and fanciful in shape; nature fairly run wild in the eccentricity of their outline; those far back in the country preserving more rounded and placid proportions. The former threw open all their beauties, their rich brown sides, their ragged declivities, their palm-tree gorges, and their white-house specks; while the latter kept a more distant and dignified reserve. Right in front of us, at some twenty miles distance, was the "Serra de Pas d'Assucar" (Sugar-Loaf Hill) which marks the mouth of the harbour, and the last of another mass of mountains to the left, if any thing more rugged and fanciful than their fellows, and flanked by little light-house-crested-islands, around which a few lazy sails were hanging. A land smell too—a smell that told of orange groves, of cocoa trees, of spices, of rich fat earth teeming with vegetation came off the coast to refresh our senses, wearied and sickened with six weeks of tar and bilge-water. Never was salvolatile to hysterical nerves, or highly seasoned ragout to eager epicure so consoling, so highly prized, so suggestive of good things in store, as that spicy breeze was to us. It made us look with contempt on the tea without milk, the

o

bread without sweetness, the fish without anything but saltness, which formed that morning's meal; we had sniffed of better things and our hitherto keenly relished fare was rejected with scorn. We were soon in our cabins preparing for shore, and it was with no little pleasure that I threw aside the checked shirt and the old tweed trowsers and slippers, my entire costume for six weeks, to appear once more in the habiliments of ordinary life. When I went on deck I could scarcely recognize the rusty shabby figure of Mons. L. of yesterday in the brilliant little creation of to-day, shining in all the tightly-strapped beauty of lavender trowsers, which covered all but the tips of the shiniest boots, with a shirt front bristling with a perfect little artillery of studs, chains, and frills, and a coat of well brushed brightness tightly fitting on to one of the smallest of waists. His portly friend the Doctor, too, was another being. His large black whiskers and moustache were fiercely pomatumed and curled and dressed, and as he was in all the stomachic grandeur of an ample and spotless white waistcoat he, looked most imposing. Mr. B. the American, having been told that a number of his countrymen *en route* to California, had taken care to preserve their bearded individuality during their stay in Rio some months before, had determined to do likewise; so that all Brasilians might know his intimate connection with the Republic. He was, however, persuaded out of this whim, and at last showed in the black satin waistcoat and "pants" which his countrymen so much delight in. By the middle of the day, all signs of wind had departed, and as the tide floated us heavily into the harbour, we had full leisure to feast our eyes on the slowly appearing beauties around us. Shining white villas gradually opened on to us, from behind the sides of rugged hills—men fishing along the coast amongst a long fringe work of gentle breakers became visible, and the numerous buildings and shipping at the upper end of the harbour told us still more distinctly that our voyage had come to an end. At about three P.M. we drifted under the famous Sugar Loaf Hill which [illegible]ds sentinel like over the mouth of the harbour.

Both sides of the bay were heavily fortressed, one battery behind the Sugar Loaf showing itself on the left, and a great fort bristling with artillery guarding the right. On passing this fort, we were hailed by a stentorian voice which we found by a telescope, to proceed from out of a man perched in a white turret, asking whence we came, our name, and "How long out;" all which enquiries the Captain seemed to answer satisfactorily, as our examiner wished us a "*bon voyage*," a conventional compliment of his which was hoarsely though kindly delivered. This presiding genius of the turret is often put to much inconvenience, for sometimes when the wind blows fresh inland, five or six vessels will pass the fort together, and he has just one minute to put this trio of questions to each, and collect the answers as conveyed through each of their speaking-trumpets, all playing on him at once. Hence his investigations are sometimes most vague and unsatisfactory. After this complimentary fort there is another on the opposite side, of a totally different nature, the business of whose inmates it is to stop all vessels from going further up the bay, than the laws of Custom Houses and Quarantine allow. If, therefore, some unlucky stranger, ignorant of harbour-rules, thrusts his bowsprit one inch beyond the line of demarcation, great guns loaded not with a charge of grape or chain, but with what is often more intensely galling, a charge of five dollars per shot, are fired as fast as the counting-house artillery men can *spunge* and load, till the erring captain is brought to a sense of his situation, and discovers that he must let go his anchor, or find himself taken to jail and his ship confiscated to pay the amount of this silent but yet warm reception.

CHAPTER XIII.

> "All hail to the Isle where the Parasite clings,
> Round the stems of the giants of ages;
> Where the rich moths and butterflies plume their bright wings,
> Where the sun in his might ever rages!"

ARRIVAL IN PORT—THE TWO COMMISSIONS—OUR LANDING—THE EMPEROR'S TURN-OUT—SCENE FROM MY BED-ROOM—CUSTOM-HOUSE WORK—THE PESTILENCE—SAIL ACROSS THE BAY—RIDE TO THE INN—THE HOSTELRIE—THE STORE-SHOP—A WASH—ASCENT OF THE MOUNTAIN.

Our Captain, being an old hand, dropped his anchor at the right time, and we had ample leisure to look around us. The upper end of the bay had just opened out upon us, and we could see a splendid sheet of water dotted with islands extending to a low green shore, over which towered ranges upon ranges of mountains, till they died away in the far distance. On the left, at the foot of some green conical hills, stood the town, yellow and irregular, and had it not been for a few stray cupolas and some handsome facades on the banks of the harbour, it might have been pronounced as ugly on the whole, but in such a situation, with such hills in its rear, and such a glorious waste of waters in its front, the dreariest combination of brick and morter, nay even a solitary Albert Gate House would lose half its unsightliness. The opposite side of the bay revels in the same profuseness of shape and colour; in some places the hills are green to their very summits, and in others they display rocky sides extending down to the very water's edge. After lying at anchor for about a quarter of an hour, we were boarded by the Sanitary Commission, which arrived in a large boat rowed by a dozen negroes, in the incarnate shape of a little brown man with spectacles, an M.D. who after a stay of a few minutes satisfied himself as to the state of our healths, and left us to the mercies of the Passport Commission. This commission came dressed in the blue coat and gold band of authority and accompanied by the captain of the port. Their investigation was not quite so happy, for amongst four passengers, only two passports could be mustered, Mr. B. and myself being the defaulters. I had omitted applying for mine through sheer carelessness, Mr. B. through a profound contempt for all the trammels and restrictions that any foreign nation could impose on an American. However we contrived to satisfy the commission, whose legs were twice in imminent danger from the rat-destroying fangs of our bull-terrier, and when he had retired, the Captain had one of the boats launched, and after a pull of some half an hour, during which we had to make a detour of respect past the bow of a great Black-Guard Boat (join the two words if you like, it would only be giving the people on board their due) moored in the middle of the harbour, for the purpose of stopping any merchandize that ship boats might convey on shore to the detriment of the Imperial Treasury. It was rapidly growing dark when we landed at the wharf, amongst a dark throng of negro boatmen, clamouring and dabbling about on the edge of the water. From some dingy oil-lamps (gas here is only mentally contemplated as yet) we could see that we were in front of a large hotel, round the entrance to which, numerous loungers in straw hats and white trowsers were taking their evening cigar and stroll. Soon a coffee-room with its glittering array of glasses and rapid waiters beamed upon us, and I was once more in the enjoyment of a comfortable tea, and deep in the back files of the *Globe* and *Times*, the latest copy of which was nearly seven weeks old. The yellow fever has been carrying off its scores of victims here lately, in spite of the vaunted superiority of this climate. It made its appearance some four months ago, and has turned the town into a house of mourning. I consequently determined on proceeding to Petropolis, a place of resort amongst the mountains, alike, for fearful people, new comers like myself, and those whose lately shaven heads gave strong proof, how nearly they had fallen victims to the fever themselves; and did not return to the town till the glorious eighteenth of June. If the Duke has as hot a-day at Apsley House as I have here now, to entertain the damaged veterans who yearly cluster round his mahogany to discuss deeds of thirty-five years ago and Port a little older, his good humour and hospitality will be put to a severe test. It is here called the depth of winter, a state of profundity which does not at all make me anxious to try the depth of summer. We soon learnt that we had arrived on the evening of a grand fete, i.e. Corpus Christi, at which Don Pedro II. had assisted, and had condescended to sully his imperial upper leathers with the dust of the city, as he marched in procession holding one corner of the host, amidst the Vivas of the citizens and the thunders of the forts. We had heard occasional cannon in the morning while out in the bay, but as the Captain remarked that "*whenever a royal baby cuts a tooth, they allus blazes away,*" we had not thought much of it: but this had been one of the grandest ever known, and a great deal of popular excitement was lingering about the streets and exploding in corners, in the shape of fireworks. It had been intended for the Emperor to have wound up the day's performances, by going to the theatre in state, but yellow fever had been busy amongst the opera troupe, the buffo and the primo tenore had fallen victims, and the prima donna was threatened with it that very night, so that the performances were "unavoidably postponed." On passing up one of the streets, I saw the Emperor's carriage waiting for him in an entry. It was one of the old double-coach pattern still to be met with about Russell-square; there had never been much attempt at ornament about it, in fact, rather less than is to be met with when an encumbered High Sheriff turns out to meet the justices, and what still remained on the panels had been badly polished and kept up. The vehicle was drawn by six mules backed by three postilions booted up to their middles, and the rest of their persons covered with tarnished gold lace put on like dabs of butter, or hanging about them in shreds. Poor fellows, they must have had a tedious day of it, for they quite groaned in their boots as I passed by them. Around the carriage were numerous satellites, footmen dressed out in all the panoply of the profession; but dignity and calves were sadly wanting, and dreary contrasts they were to the heroes of our great flunkeyographer, Thackeray. I had heard so much of centipedes, scorpions, and of other creeping things peculiar to the Brazils, that I got little sleep the first night, for dreams of animals with heads like dragons and no end of legs, flitting about, sadly haunted me. All these terrors vanished with the sun which was shining hotly and brightly upon the Laryo de Paco (Palace Square) just under my window. Here I looked upon an animated scene, a large open space was before me, bounded on the right by the water, on the brink of which numerous boats with their clamorous crews and owners were drawn up ready for custom. On the left was the Palace, the town residence of the Emperor, but which he has carefully avoided during the last three months of fever. Around its portico were files of soldiers, mostly undersized mulattoes, with caps by many degrees more unsightly than our own "Alberts," drawn up for morning parade. The space in the middle was filled up by a varied crowd. There were merchants hurrying to morning's business under the shade of green, blue, and red umbrellas, half-naked negroes staggering along at a shuffling trot under enormous burdens, each one chaunting or arguing to himself, by way of beguiling the time;—negro women, with their dusky offspring bound to them by shawls of every hue; beggars in everybody's way displaying their deformities, and boatmen seizing hold of every passer-by, at all likely to prove customers. The whole of that day I spent in getting my luggage passed or rather seized at the Customs, for of late some severe reforms have been made amongst the douaniers here, and ten or fifteen milreas, by the aid of which, judiciously administered, whole packages might some months since have passed unscathed, have now lost their potency, and I had to witness the dearest interests of my portmanteau violated. Every book from two great volumes of essays down to the smallest keepsake were taken, and I began (such is the low tone of morality that travellers acquire) to detest their very honesty. One man especially disgusted me, a fat man in authority who had been with me across the bay to the ship, a long way certainly, but he was so amiable, had listened so calmly and politely to my bad Portuguese, had pointed me out so affably every place of interest, had accepted of my hospitality (i. e.) such as a temperance ship afforded, and had perspired so good naturedly all the time, that I thought I had secured a partisan ; but lo, he turned upon and rent my shirts and trowsers like a savage, pointing out suspicious corners that no eye but his would have detected. A French gentleman, a person of very questionable trunks, had his effects looked over before mine, and though it was an investigation of three-quarters of an hour, yet it was highly amusing. It was a great treat to see the searcher, without exception the blandest man I ever saw, quietly unwrapping waistcoats, disembowelling pairs of stockings, plunging into all sorts of secret places, and extracting without fail at every dive, gloves, pieces of valuable stuffs, smelling bottles of filagree work, and jewelled gimcracks, the latest notions of the Rue St. Honore or Palais Royal. The enraged owner meantime was in that state, produced by a Brazilian sun acting upon French choler, more easily fancied than described, and in a moment of unguarded temper pitched an old shoe at his persecutor, and mockingly inquired the duty upon it. The bland man smiling all the time took it up, examined it, and producing from the toe an unsuspected piece of soap, quietly put it by amongst the other confiscated articles. After that the Frenchman sank entirely, and got into a state of stupor from which he was only aroused by some one knocking his hat off, he having unconsciously covered himself in the Imperial Customhouse. The talk of every one was of yellow fever. From Bahia had come that tropical scourge, unsuspected, unfeared, and had surprised in all its malignancy this climate, for years the boast of its inhabitants as the perfection of healthiness. Three months ago it made its first appearance, and since then had been weeping and wailing—business for a time was paralyzed—every family had lost some of its most valued ornaments—funerals could not be furnished quick enough—doctors had dreadfully differed, and the scourge had carried them off in the midst of their bickerings—whole ships crews had given in,—the houses of the largest merchants had been closed. One of them had every clerk and negro in the house ill at the same time, and he, the head of the house, used to flee the house of sickness in the evening, with the keys in his pocket, and to open the warehouse, and take down the shutters himself in the morning, while his day would be spent between the coffee wharf and his sick charges, for one or two of whom he had to order coffins beforehand. One of the principal refuges from this enemy was a beautiful retreat, called Petropolis, amongst the Orgao mountain range, about thirty miles from the town, and the residence of the Emperor. Thither did my friends despatch me immediately on my arrival, for many new comers had fallen victims, and it was not thought safe to stay longer than necessary in a place where there was still danger. On the next morning, therefore, regretting I had seen so little of a place so strange and so beautiful, I found myself on board a little steamboat bound for the above-mentioned place. Like every Saturday's steamer in large towns, the deck was crowded with a miscellaneous company. There were imperial couriers, booted and spurred;—English fathers, of the true Margate cut, loaded with parcels, and glad to change the dust and infection of the town for the pure air, breathed by their families in the mountains;—English mothers, a welcome sight again after eight months, feeding groups of children, of all sizes, out of baskets, while a passive and burdened papa would be sitting at a distance;—invalids, whose jaundiced faces and lately shaven heads showed how sharp had been the struggle with them;—wild looking men in large sombreros and tassels and yellow boots, decorated with highly ornamented spurs;—change seekers of every nation;—servants, sailors, and negroes, were all huddled together under a scanty awning, which was but a slight protection from a sun of 90

P

degrees. Our way pointed towards the upper end of the bay, and as we cleared out of the numerous ships and from behind the Ilha das Colras, nearly the whole of that magnificent sheet of water was opened to us, presenting an expanse of some twenty miles. Islands of every sort and size were scattered about, some nothing more than a fantastic assemblage of round stones, the abode of penguins and sea-gulls ; some clothed with all the rich glory of the richest vegetation, while on others habitations had been built among palms and orange trees. Right before us, extending from east to west, was the giant range of the Orgaos mountains, to which we were bound, while behind us, towering over the city, less imposing, but more marked, was the Corcovado range, which had been most prominent on our first entrance into the bay. Two hours' sail brought us to the opposite side of the bay and to the mouth of a little river, the banks of which were covered by a rich green cane jungle, along the bottom of which glanced kingfishes of every colour, while a few houses, with low red roofs, here and there, showed that man had not quite given way to vegetation. After an hour's twisting and turning we came to a little port, and there was an immediate rush of all on board to secure mules and conveyances for further progress. A friend I had met on the way, an American merchant dressed like a quaker, tall and scant, distanced everybody in the race, and through his knowledge of the language and other good offices, I found myself and three others in a sege, or sort of two-wheeled vehicle, like which I have seen nothing in England, not even amongst the numerous dusty equipages a country inn turns out on a fair day, or amongst the numerous cab inventions that have racked the bones of Londoners for the last twenty years. It was something like a small stage-coach turned wrong side up, and nobody could enter without the rest of the occupants standing up and severely bumping their heads against the roof. For eight miles along a road thorougly flat, dusty and English, were we taken, passing on our way strings of mules coming from the interior, loaded with coffee (every mule taking 8 arrobas of 32lbs. each), and accompanied by two or more negroes, who seemed to be going on their way rejoicing, as every one of them invariably sang. We saw, also, two or three Ranchoes, the resting places of the cavalcade, where the beasts shed their burdens and are turned out to graze for the night, and the muleteers building for themselves little huts of the luggage, and lying on skins, enjoy themselves with their cheroots and cachaca (rum). An hour's drive brought us to an inn at the foot of the mountains, but the clouds which we had seen from a distance playing about their tops had now thickened and descended, and meeting the mists rising from the low country, had enveloped everything in obscurity. There was soon a general caparisoning and "mounting in hot haste" of mules, and all the steam-boat people, who by that time had arrived, began busily covering themselves with poncho cloaks, getting into minas boots, and striving with unruly spur buckles. As, from the beauty of the morning, I had not anticipated the necessity of cloaks and boots, and my luggage had not arrived, I was obliged to stay all night, and my companions, on mules or in litters—cloaks, boots, and all—were soon hidden in the mist. My hostelrie was certainly none of the best, for it laboured under the disadvantage of a landlord above his business, a fact he used practically to evince, by looking out of the window of a handsome room upstairs (which he seldom left) upon his guests, who were left to complain in a dirty unfinished apartment below, where luggage and saddle housings, poultry and market stuff, occupied one corner, while the guests sat, ate, and slept in the other. Next to the inn was an immense general store for the accommodation of the interior of the country, where returning mules called and carried back into the coffee-region every necessity and luxury. The shop could well supply them, as Manchester, Birmingham, Sheffield, London, and America, seemed to have contributed to the stock; for everything—muskets or muslins, pens or castor oil, umbrellas or butter, were there. Day and Martin, with an immense picture of the house in Holborn, on a large placard, occupied a place on one wall, and Lea and Perrin's Worcestershire Sauce attracted attention from the other. Despite of the general bad attendance, a French gentleman, who came in wet through during the evening—the exact likeness of Mr. Harley, and who conducted himself exactly as that elderly comedian would under the same circumstances—and myself, managed to get an excellent supper on eggs and gallinha, the stock dish of the country, and then retired to such beds as the house afforded: but various conflicting emotions, or rather *flea*motions, kept me long awake. The next morning the mountains stood before us in all their clear grandeur, showing a splendid barrier of green. They were of various heights, but all of the same round shape, and covered with the same foliage. The morning sun was now upon them, and they were lit up gloriously. After treating myself to a good wash, in a bucket—a thing no less pleasing to myself than to the inmates of the hotel, who, guests, shopmen, blacks, and all, had come to look on, and had formed a ring round me during the operation, finishing by generally borrowing my pocket-comb,—I got out a mule of promising appearance, and began the ascent. "Mr. Harley," who could by no means keep himself still except when asleep, and then he snored, had been up some time before, and had set off on his journey in a different direction. My road was the perfection of a road in every sense; the craggy base of the hill on one side running over with gushing water-courses, and on the other a deep gorge of trees, whose tops, with their immense branches alive with numerous birds and glancing with butterflies, drooped over, so as entirely to shade one from the morning sun. Parrots, green and black, many little widow birds, and others of gayer hue, flew above, a general chirrup surrounded me, and the inspiriting shouts of the muleteers thrown back from the neighbouring hill, echoed around as they urged their toiling troops up the mountains above. My mule, who evinced less disposition to share in the general cheerfulness than I to dispute the question with him, I dismissed by a returning black, and with those happy assistants, a sound foot and a good stick, went on alone. On my way I passed little white flat-roofed houses, at the doors of which were many groups engaged on their Sunday toilet, here and there a way side Figaro would be plying his scissors and his tongue, while from many a window the sallow face but dark gleaming eye of the Brazilian peasant girl would look a serious greeting. After two hours walk I found myself at the top of the mountain and near the entrance of the gorge, on which stands the town of Petropolis. On turning round here, what a prospect met me! The place was surnamed the Boa Vista.

CHAPTER XIV.

Under this cloud I walk, gentlemen; pardon my rude assault. I am a traveller, who, having surveyed many of the terrestrial angles of this globe, am hither arrived to peruse this little spot.—*Christmas Ordinary.*

SCENE FROM THE BOA VISTA—THE EMPEROR'S PALACE AND PERSON—THE BABY NUISANCE—A FEMALE SKETCH—A YORKSHIREMAN—TOOTHPICKS—BRAZILIAN FORESTS—CARD PLAYING—TIME KILLING—DR. * * *—MY DEPARTURE.

The Boa Vista, on which I found myself, was ranked high amongst the numerous Boa Vistas which the country affords. From an altitude of 3000 feet I could mark every step of my course since leaving Rio de Janeiro. The town itself (30 miles away) just discernible from the presence of something yellow—the glorious bay between, dotted by its hundred islands, and from which the mists of the previous night had not yet cleared away, but had combined themselves into thick snow flakes, and lingered about as if unwilling to leave such a fairy resting-place—the low rich country between the bay and the hill teeming with verdure—the winding road from the inn along which I had just come showing its red course at intervals—all my track was marked out. On the other side of the city was the giant ridge of mountains, with the Gavia, the Coacovado, Tejuca Peak, and the Páo do Assucar, a magnificent assemblage, prominent and striking, while through an occasional opening was the blue sea, the soft and distant limit of this magnificent scene. It was with difficulty that I could leave this place, but soon after I began to approach a town, and "Hotel Frances" and "Hotel Braganza" told me I was not far from my journey's end. Petropolis is a long straggling village, with a stream running through the middle, and completely surrounded by hills. In the middle, upon rising ground, is the Emperor's palace. I had expected that something like privacy, if not splendour, would have characterised this country residence of the grandson of Dom João, but there was nothing of the sort. No massive gates emblazoned and surly-portered, no iron railings, no trees, no guards were there, nothing to keep the *profanum vulgus* from looking in at the windows or walking in at the front door, while Majesty was dining or lounging; or while it was taking an evening stroll, or from running after it or dogging it in the Brighton fashion. About the middle of the town, just in the situation that public baths and reading rooms would occupy in a watering-place, is the Imperial retreat, a long unfinished building of one story, the exact pattern of the refreshment rooms in a new railway town, where three or four railways choose to meet, and where some hundred passengers are to be dined daily. From a little chapel, a number of peasantry were issuing, and after them came the Emperor himself, a tall and rather stout young man, with a slight stoop. He has a long face, with good features, and a light beard and whiskers, and when he took off his hat, a good round forehead was exhibited. He has a mild expression of features, but rather childish and submissive, and not exactly indicative of the sort of mind calculated to keep under and together the many turbulent intriguing spirits that encircle his throne. A short cut over a hill brought me to the hotel whither I had been recommended, as one of the best in the town, and much frequented by English and Americans: one end had been glassed in and intended for a conservatory, but air plants and orchids had given place to gentlemen with cigars, and the only plant the least attended to in it was the tobacco. What first struck me was the great quantity of babies and small children that rolled about the entrance, one could scarcely walk without seriously injuring an infant, and there was one gloriously fat child called Gracey, that made a universal stumbling block of itself but never got hurt, and what is more, never cried. Shortly after my arrival, I made a dreadful mistake about my bed-room door, it being, like six others in a long passage, painted green, and before I could step I got into a colony of nurses and children of all sizes, and I never remember to have witnessed such a scene of trussing up, powdering, napkining, and noise as was there going on. At three o'clock the guests began to muster, not for dinner, but to talk about dinner, a little ceremony which took place daily, when the negligence of making dinner an hour late was talked over and inveighed against with much eloquence and warmth till four, when dinner did come, and I had an opportunity of seeing my companions. It was served on a long table in a long room, the top being the American and the bottom the English end, a slight sprinkling of French and Germans occupying the middle. Opposite to me was a pretty brunette of about thirty-five, in ringlets, who kept up a continual artillery of ogles and glances, not at any one person in particular, but at everybody generally. She was a woman of great talkative powers, which were greatly enhanced by a lisp. Her great topic was a certain A—, whom she called "her A—," who hadn't come when he ought to have come, or who was coming at some unknown time, which rather excited one's curiosity. However, next Saturday, A— did come, with a batch of husbands from the city, in the shape of a magnificent Hebrew in spectacles, and the meeting which I was fortunate enough to witness, was an interesting, if not an affecting incident. She seemed to have a great admirer in a feeble looking young man, a late convalescent from the fever, who hung upon her words, and took wine with her at least four times during dinner. But the most pleasant sight was the beaming face of an Englishman at the bottom of the table, Yorkshire all over; it was written in every line of his rosy countenance, but when the mouth opened and the unshackled Doric of that county flowed out, right delicious was it to an ear accustomed to nine months of American nasology. From this gentleman, who never looked serious once during my three weeks in the place, in fact, I doubt his ability of doing so at any time, I learnt a good deal about the people in the house, their virtues, their little failings, their deeds, their misdeeds, their likings, and their dislikings. He was a great wag too, and had a quiet vein of banter by which he would bring peo-le out, make them commit themselves, and then have a fit of scarlet convulsions behind their backs to the intense amusement of the lookers-on. He was also very polite to the ladies, and his way of begging for "that pretty little waltz" was quite irresistible. Our dinner was of the rough, heavy, and ready school; for, after two courses had been disposed of, an immense joint of roast beef at one end and a leg of mutton at the other were brought on as a species of light refection; after which, gentlemen, ladies, and all beguiled the time with toothpicks, a custom of the country into which foreigners fall with surprising facility. Amongst Americans it was nothing out of the common way, but I was sorry to see two or three of my pretty countrywomen, late arrivals, take to it *con amore*. After the toothpicks, the American end got up and departed, leaving the English to enjoy their cheese and port wine with their half-hour's sit afterwards. This national contrast was illustrated daily without fail. I soon began to be acquainted with all my companions, and on fine days the time was spent agreeably enough—the mornings in rambles and rides about the forests by which we were surrounded, and an hour's walk would take us into the depths of woods, where every feature of Brazilian vegetation was to be met with. Although it was the depth of winter no change was worked in the universal green, but every thing seemed as fresh as on an English May morning; the few flowers that remained would have been the ornaments of endless English hot houses, straggling and uncared for though they seemed there. Parasites of every shape, cipos of every size, hung and clustered about their magnificent props, as if striving in their youth and strength to succour and cherish the old friend who had borne them up so bravely in their infancy. Occasional, monkeys, active and chattering, would just show themselves aloft, and then disappear. A step in some low hurried corner would disturb moths of indescribable brilliancy, but pursuit would be stopped by that mysterious rustling in the brushwood which told that some creeping enemy, angry and venomous, had been dis-

-turbed also, and warned the unwary foot from staying longer in such dangerous precincts. In the evening a round game at cards was our usual practice, into which the ladies entered with great gusto, and made up little partnerships amongst sisters, to the great disturbance of any milreas lying loose in the pockets of gentlemen. At one game particularly (Pacaie), the lady with the ringlets was a most noted player; she could take the whole management into her hands, correct mistakes, instruct ignorance, sell her own "fish" judiciously, buy to great advantage of a French gentleman who was a constant loser, keep down the rising tempers of two ladies of the Jewish persuasion, one stout and the other thin, who always disagreed about calculations, to our intense delight, console gentlemen who got up losers, and withal manage to get unto herself a perfect little fortune of milrea notes, the result of industry and discretion. Wet days nevertheless tired us severely; for when it does begin to rain in the Brazils it keeps it up, and mud accumulates prodigiously. Our only literature was a volume of the *Illustrated News* for 1844, which had been well thumbed and digested; in fact I don't think there was one of us who could not tell exactly the shape of every triumphal arch under which the Queen is depicted to have travelled on her Scotch tour, in that interesting volume. This could only serve for two at a time, the pianoforte for two more and a hanger on, the cribbage board and the whist table for but eight the most, both of which were always in full employment after breakfast, while the remaining thirty odd had to concentrate their energies on cigars, a bagatelle table or their bed-rooms, and with these managed to keep themselves up till dinner time. One of our most notable characters was a stout little gentleman of about sixty, who had acquired the sobriquet of "Doctor," but had I not known that he was a navy lieutenant on half pay I should have put him down for an admiral at least; he had all the heartiness, the good humour, and broad jest of the "Most Noble Commander" school of men. Originally brought up for the faculty, he had quitted it for the sea, had been all over the world, and had known personally many of our naval stars at the beginning of this century. He had practised his original calling whenever the service required it, during which time he had seen disease and death in every shape, and had dreadfully incensed the profession both in England and this place, by curing people whom they had given up, for which he was of course called a "know-nothing." He had lived for some time in the neighbourhood of Peckham Rye, where he had contracted a great horror for the fervid evening style of preaching to be met with in the neighbourhood of Champion Hill, and had incensed his wife and pastor dreadfully by resolutely snoring out sermons, to hear which, ardent ladies, on hot summer nights, from Clapham, Holloway, and Kennington, had crushed and fainted. He had come out to this climate for change of air, and was on the eve of a journey to the Minas district to superintend a large estate until his return home. He had a great faculty of knowing something about everybody, and his friendship with a naval connexion of mine brought us together wonderfully. He certainly was one of the chief ornaments of our society there, for who could make a dull half-hour lively like he, (i. e.) when not a victim to back-gammon? Who could tell such amusing stories at dinner? Who like him could lead off a quadrille, where his buff waistcoat and short legs were seen in the thickest of the *ronde finale*—and who when taken ill would cause so many enquiries, and have such levees in a little bed-room, which also served for a dispensary as the general favorite, Dr. Y——. Reports of rapidly declining fever quickly thinned our ranks at the hotel, and every morning joyous parties of people strapped, buckled, and booted, would be setting off after breakfast for the ride down the mountain, and as mistakes and delays about mules and luggage were always being made, it was often the next day before the city was reached. Indeed, in one case, that of a very stout young Scotchman, of something over 17 stone, exclusive of boots, and accompanied by a pretty little wife, it was something like a matter of sixty hours from the time of departure before they reached their destination; in fact

I walked my beautiful way down the mountain again two days after they had left, and caught them up in the steamboat, which bore me back to Rio.

CHAPTER XV.

"Large constellations burning, mellow moons and happy skies,
Breadths of tropic shade and palms in cluster, knots of Paradise.
Droops the heavy blossom'd bower, hangs the heavy fruited tree—
Summer isles of Eden lying in dark purple spheres of sea."

TENNYSON.

CONTRAST BETWEEN SLAVES IN RIO AND THE STATES—A DRINK MUDDLE—ASCENT OF THE CORCOVADO—SCENE THEREFROM—SAILORS—CATHOLIC CHAPELS—THE PRIMA DONNA—HOUSE ECONOMY—IRON FOUNDRIES—ENGINEERS' CHIT-CHAT—NATIVE VIEWS OF CRICKET.

The thing which first struck me in Rio was the immense number of blacks, who are to be seen in every corner of the streets. Though many are to be met with in the States, they do not give one the idea of being in such a degraded state as they are in this country. Slavery is slavery everywhere; but here it stalks abroad, branded, diseased, and naked. It is sometimes difficult to fancy the black of the Southern States as a slave, when on Sundays he turns out in the gayest clothes and the gayest spirits of anybody, or when his never-tiring foot or fiddle is devoted to the service of some dark Dinah or Susannah, at a ball. But here slavery has none of these disguises; it flourishes in all its dreadful loathsomeness and misery. Amongst that squalid group in the corner of yonder street, with baskets besides them, waiting to be hired, all is subdued and silent. They don't seem to feel their situation, for they have long grown callous to it; but you never hear, as you would among a similar group in the States, the merry jest, the animated discussion about nothing, or the noisy laugh that convulses every part of the body at once. They bow their heads despondingly in the sun, seemingly conscious of nothing. The finest race of blacks in the country are the Minas; they are easily distinguished from the rest by their fine stature, jet black colour, and a mark branded on their nose. They are sometimes six feet in height, and the women tall in proportion. When they first come from the coast they have a lofty appearance and a sort of noble bearing, which a month in a slave ship could not subdue, but a year's staggering under heavy burdens makes them quite different creatures. The women have a peculiar soft eye and a long eye-lash. The other tribes are not easily distinguishable, being all of the woolly-headed and flat-nosed Mongolian family. There is a capital way here of punishing a negro who has been guilty of intoxication. He is not locked up, as in that case he would be of no use to his master, but they only put his head in gaol, while his limbs and body have free exercise; and a most effectual kind of incarceration it is too. A grim sort of iron head-piece, half mask and half helmet, is put on, and chub-blocked behind. Two holes are made in it for the eyes and two for the nostrils. It is perfectly impossible for him to drink anything through this "helmet barred," and he goes about an object of derision amongst his fellow-workmen, and a striking example of the effects of "the bottle." I think a hint might be taken from this in old England. There is no place in the world more calculated to make one set out on little expeditions than Rio de Janeiro, for which ever way you shape your course, be it to the mountains, the sea, or the bay, you will be abundantly rewarded. Boa Vistas await you at every turn. Perhaps, for a generally comprehensive view, that from the top of the Corcovado is the most distinguished. It is four or five miles from the town, and the way to it skirts the great aqueduct, one of the most striking works in the place. It was built by the Jesuits, and is an invaluable convenience to the inhabitants. The best start is made from the Santa Theresa Hill, where the aqueduct leaves the arches that carry it over the lower streets, and twines its way up to the mountains along a seemingly low yellow wall, often hidden in thorn and brushwood. Taking this wall as your guide, you are led along a beautiful winding course up the wooded-side of the hill, that forms the connecting link between the little green morros of the city and the grand mountain chain of the Gavia. The way has all the delightful characteristics of Brasilian scenery, its drooping boughs, its luxuriant undergrowth, its butterflies, its birds, with occasional peeps at distance. Soon the little road gets more steep and rugged, and girt in by trees; and your horse, which hitherto has done his work wonderfully, begins to show such decided signs of inability, that it becomes necessary to tie him up and leave him. Half an hour's scramble ensues, and then you are ushered out of the obscurity in which you have been labouring, on to a broad slippery rock surmounted by a flag staff; whence, on the top of the mighty Corcovado, from a nearly perpendicular altitude of 3000 feet, you have your reward a hundred-fold. I have seen the principal views in the Highlands, have been a lingering worshipper of the distance from Stirling and Edinburgh Castle, have "climbed the dark brow of the mighty Helvellyn," and traced the windings of the lordly Hudson from the top of Kaatskills, but every one of them "pales its ineffectual fire" before this panorama. Every natural excellence, wood and sea, lake and mountain, sun and cloud, seem here to have put forth their greatest efforts, to form one grand harmonious whole. It is perfection itself. Every feature from the white sail in the extreme distance, darting back in diamond glances the reflection of the morning sun, on the one side, to the fleecy cloud just pausing on the highest peak of the Orgao mountains on the other, all seem to have combined to do honour to one of nature's choicest pictures. The Sugar-loaf Hill at the entrance of the harbour which frowned so fiercely on us, as we passed under him, looks now what it is called, a mere sugar loaf. The immense three-decked "Vasquez de Gama," which looked a very whale in the bay amongst the rest of her floating sisters, is now insignificant indeed, while the whole of the bay, with all its islands, its nooks, and its windings, is revealed as if on a map. Oh, that some great Mogul of patrons, some mighty Augustus of the age, could influence a Lee, a Turner, and a Burford, or a like trio, to pitch their tent here for a month, that Englishmen might form some very faint idea of what richness, what form, what splendour, has been lavished upon this land! Here is nothing to alloy the unmoved pleasure of the scene, nothing to make one think that there is any misery, or squalor, or sickness, or death, within reach of you. Everything from the mountain top to the distant horizon, from the sun to the faintest sea ripple, seem to illustrate one great scene of peace, repose, and love. Minutes pass quickly away here, and dosing and musing will go together. It was therefore pleasant to be aroused from such dreaminess, but nothing could sound more pleasantly by way of awakener, than the peal of many English voices, which began to be heard in joyful jargon, and two or three minutes brought up to the rock a lot of English officers and middies, from an H.B.M. in the bay. One of them, (no Masons or Mc. Donoughs ride so boldly as sailors when they do get outside a horse) had brought up his beast to the top, a feat of no little peril, but which gave great enjoyment to all concerned. It was curious to see how silent they all were on the first glance at the prospect, then penknives were produced, and some terrible mutilations having been committed on the flag-staff, in the endeavour to cut our initials, we all went down together. The principal street for shops in the town is the Rua d'Ouvidor, and all the owners are French people; in fact, it reminds you much of an uncovered Burlington Arcade, only a little wider and a good deal dirtier. The fronts are much the same size, and music shops alternate with hair-dressers, shoemakers, and modistes, in much the same ratio. At the top of the Rua is the Square of Francisco di Paulo, called so from the large church, the most striking object in it. There is nothing, however, in this church, or indeed in any other one in the city worthy of notice, and all of them are more than usually tawdry and staring. On the shrines, everything like good taste has been perfectly borne down with coarse gilding and "loud" colour. The figure of the Virgin Mary suggests immediately that of the young lady who accompanies Jack o' the Green, with a ladle on the first of May. In vain you look for some Incarnation picture or Holy Family of any value, as one would have thought from the proximity of Portugal to the land of Murillo and Campana, that some gem of those great masters or at least some good copies would have found their way over at the time of the Imperial immigration; but no, the altar pieces are very few, and those of a very inferior character. The next Square to Francisco de Paulo is the Largo do Theatro. The Theatre itself is very large, but dreadfully dingy and badly lighted. Operas are generally given, but very often long five act plays, which the Brazilians must think the perfection of dreariness. The Prima Donna of the Opera troupe is very much run after, and has turned the heads of many young men to such an extent that nearly half a newspaper column is daily devoted to their productions, addressed to "The Queen of Song," and the like invocations. I saw her in Linda di Chamouni, and she seemed to repay these infatuated offerings by the number of nods and smiles, that Thillon-like, she lavished on the delighted pit. Her singing would entitle her to a good place as a second Donna at either of the Operas in England. The present tenor, who was lately elevated to the situation of primo, by the death of his superior, is a fat elderly gentleman, and when he came on dressed in full regimentals as the gallant young officer in the last act, he illustrated the old dramatic Colonel to perfection: and as he knelt before his mistress, with his great red face, his hand on his heart, and a cropped wig on his head, he looked a sort of serious and agonised Paul Bedford, if such a thing there could be. The baritones and basses do not call for any remark, and the legs of the supernumeraries are rather worse than they generally are amongst that body of men. The principal business streets are the Ruas Direita, Alfandega, Dos Pescadores, and Quitanda. In these streets the merchants mostly live. The houses are much inferior to those in Havanna in point of size and airiness. The warehouse occupies the whole of the ground-floor, and the first-floor has generally the front for a drawing-room, the middle for the offices, and the back for dining-room. Bed-rooms are dispersed in every nook and corner above, and there is little

R

or no ceremony about callers or diners. A looker-in is always welcomed and received hospitably. The evenness of the town is broken by six hills, all surmounted by churches, and some well covered with foliage, the travelling up to which is rough, stony, and tedious, especially on hot days. About four miles off the town, across the bay, a Brazilian, one of the most influential men in Rio, has large iron-works and ship-building yards, which give employment to about six hundred people. It was curious to see men of all nations collected together there working, Germans and Negroes, French and Brazilians, were all busily employed; but the directing spirits of the establishment, those men, each of whom two or three others would be following about, obedient and ready for smelting or firing, or hammering, were easily distinguished; there was no mistaking the greasy fustian, the cap, the dirty apron, the hard riven-in lines on the smutty forehead: English or Scotch they were sure to be, and they seemed to go about conscious of their own superiority, as if they knew that no nation with any pretensions to civilisation could get on without steam, and that they were looked upon as the dispensers of all its mighty mysteries. In almost every steam-boat in the country, you see one of these iron spirits with his handful of tow and his oil-can, calmly lubricating or directing. He knows no master on board but steam, and that he bends to his will. He has an establishment of his own, and the foreman and cook wait upon him, obeying all his behests. If the Captain came to dispute with him, he would get him into such an entanglement about pistons, cranks, blow-pipes, and safety-valves, that he would soon retire discomfited. When he goes on shore he seldom dons a tail-coat, but in the everlasting blue jacket with two rows of buttons, moleskin waistcoat and trowsers, and thick shoes, he stalks about among his fellow-men, a sort of social potentate or principal ambassador of a great power, whom no one can withstand and all must perforce respect. The pay of the artisans in the foundry varies from three to six milreas (6s. 6d. to 13s.) ℔ day. One engineer in a steam-boat, with whom I had a good deal of conversation, was paid sixty dollars a month, was kept, and had an extra berth in which he could take a passenger. He said he had a very comfortable place of it, was making money, had bought two slaves, and had one under engineer and six foremen in his command to attend to a 30-horse engine, a thing two lads often manage in England. It is amusing to get down into the hot oily engine-room, and talk with these men about steam-boats and boilers; they know something of every boat that has been launched up to the last six months, and speak of their being worked by a pair of Fawcett's, or a pair of Miller's, or a pair of Napier's, as if further explanation was unnecessary. They also treasure up newspapers old and greasy, in which are accounts of feats performed by steamers, of boilers burst, or engines broken down, and pointing to the last, they would say, "Ay, sir, they was a pair of Bury's, or a pair of Todd's, I know'd they wouldn't stand that station, (it never was a pair of anybody's where they had worked) and then they would enter into an explanation about why they wouldn't stand, about how the beaming was not strong enough, and how them sort of cranks never answered nohow, and how he knew Big Bill of Newton, as had put em up," with all such mechanical lore. They seem to like much to get hold of a country man, into whose ear they can pour all their experiences and their complaints, and when he leaves will squeeze his hand in their leathery grasp as if they were squeezing a sponge, the only difference being that water comes out of his eyes instead of the thing squeezed. Their great ambition is to establish themselves in a mechanic's shop, to get their families and young apprentice acquaintances out, and to set up boiler making on their own account. Another British peculiarity here, but amongst a different class, is the fondness of cricket, but this Rio Janeiro only shares in common with every place where there is anything like a British society. It is curious that no other country really cares about national sports. In Rio, where perhaps there are more representatives of foreign countries than in any other place, there is nothing to bring together the Americans, the French, the Germans, or the Spanish. Steeple-chasing, boat-racing, and other out-door sports, are considered the peculiar property of one nation, and long may that nation enjoy that peculiarity. An excellent cricket club flourishes at Rio. At San Christopher, near the town, is a sort of common ground, where on every holiday in winter a tent is pitched. Caterers are regularly appointed to superintend the conveying of every eatable and drinkable necessary—sides are chosen, and play commences. This lasts till five, when wickets are drawn and then corks. After dinner, toasts and songs, loyal and jovial, are given and sung. The natives don't understand it at all, but come crowding about the tent, evidently trying very hard to make out about "Britons never, never shall be slaves," "The good time Coming," or "The Pope he leads a happy Life;" but I should fancy, not with much success. Their endeavours to solve the nature of a cricket-ball are often more satisfactory, as they always stand very near the wicket, and I have seen two or three slashing leg-hits disperse them and satisfy them sooner than they expected. The general conclusion they have arrived at respecting the game, is that the English who play at it are mad, and run about in the sun to catch the fever.

CHAPTER XVI.

"Yet tell me not my native skies are bleak,
That flushed with liquid wealth no cane fields wave;
For virtue pines, and manhood dare not speak,
And nature's glories brighten round the slave."

The Earl of Carlisle.

A BLOODTHIRSTY BRAZILIAN—OPERATIONS OF THE ENGLISH SLAVE CRUISERS—POETIC ATTENTIONS TO LORD PALMERSTON—A REPENTANT GOVERNMENT—PASSAGE TO RIO GRANDE—PORTUGUESE MARINERS—DESTERRO—CALIFORNIA SEA CAPTAINS—DELIGHT OF SLAVE CAPTAINS AT OUR OPPOSITION—RIO GRANDE—ITS PROPENSITY TO OX-SLAUGHTER—LASSOING AND LASSOERS—ORNITHOLOGICAL RESEARCHES.

PIRATIRIA INGLEZA was the all cry when I was leaving Rio. It had quite superseded the fever excitement, and sixty per cent. to be imposed on British goods was looked upon as inevitable. At dinner in the Brazilian merchant's house where I lived, I used to hear the question fairly discussed, and there was one blood-thirsty little man in some high government office, a frequent guest, who would argue strongly not only for sixty per cent., but also for a general stirring up of the Mulatto population to "Matar Todos Inglezes," (kill all the English,) at which most savage suggestion, the old English book-keeper of the house, who sat at the bottom of the table, would wink at me most happily, and afterwards tell me that he had heard himself and his countrymen doomed in the same way for the last five years, and was not in the least affected by it. The daily papers reported the greatest differences as prevailing in the Brazilian councils on the subject. Bursts of the most flowery and savage eloquence, in which the English were pronounced as pirates ever since the days of Drake and Frobisher,

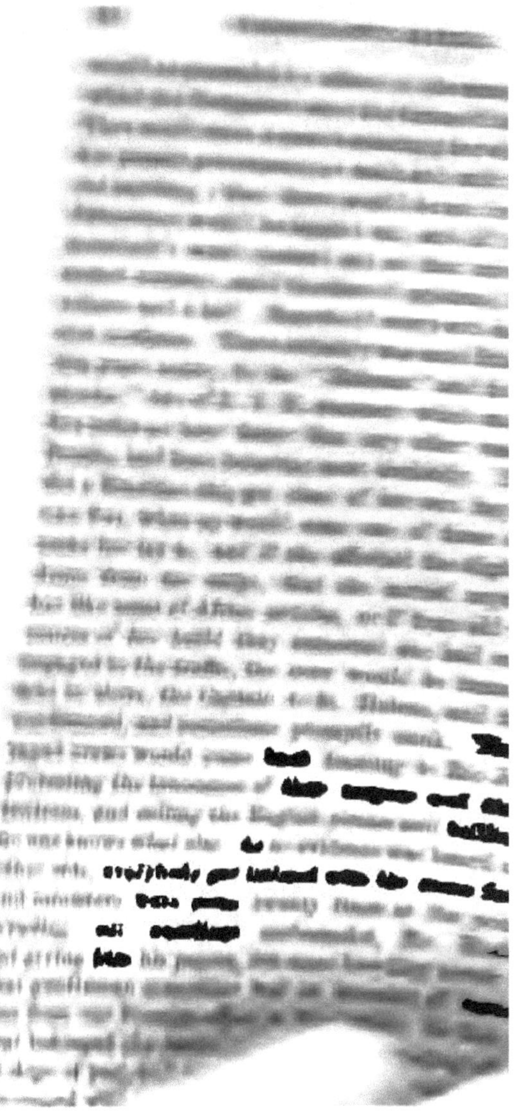

ing stanzas occupied a prominent place in the journal of the day :—

I.

The minister deems in his idle dreams
 That all to his will must bow ;
That a purpose gained, for humanity feigned,
 Fresh laurels will place on his brow.

II.

He pities the slaves ! ! why a million of graves
 Gape wide near his mansion's door ;
While treasure is drained, for humanity feigned,
 To swallow the starving poor.

III.

A patriot he ! why the Queen of the Sea
 From her empire should banish the knave,
Whose measures have gained, for humanity feigned,
 Contempt for the good and the brave.

IV.

He has tarnished the name of the nation, whose fame
 Was bright as the visions in song ;
And England has deigned, for humanity feigned,
 To stoop to injustice and wrong.

V.

The flag of our isle has floated long while,
 Nor been by the boldest defied,
Now that proud flag is stained, for humanity feigned,
 And to pirates now nearly allied. ANGLICUS.

If Lord Palmerston has not already fallen into one of the "million graves" that according to "Anglicus," gape near the doors of the Foreign-office, he will without doubt be annihilated by the tremendous satire conveyed in the above. How a purpose, a treasure, England, measures, and a proud flag could all be "Feigned for humanity" is certainly perplexing, but they say in defence of the poet, that Lord P. is capable of anything. On the day I left for Rio Grande, the governor of a fort [illegible] just arrived, in a state bordering on insanity, for the [illegible]orant" had arrived off his stronghold, and had [illegible] from under his very batteries a ship of notori[illegible] tendencies. He had fired one round of [illegible]ich one of the Cormorant's men was killed [illegible]way with his garrison, and the Cormor[illegible]nd blown his fort up. This certainly [illegible] h of power, for it had infringed one of the slave treaties, and there was no knowing where it might stop. Dull, therefore, were the forebodings of merchants with a duty of 60 per cent. staring them in the face, and an enraged Mulatto population around them. The "Southampton," fifty guns, a large war steamer, the Rifleman, Sharpshooter, and two brigs, had all come or were coming in that evening, and reports to the effect that the sinking policy was going to be tried in the bay on the "Serpente," a large steamer, were rife every where. However, this vessel had been sold in time to the Brazilian government, and the flag preserved it from any such experiment. I was since glad to hear while at Rio Grande, that everything had been settled for the present, that the government conscious of the faithless way in which it had kept its treaties for the last five years, was at last brought to see that retaliation was justifiable, and to pass measures for the immediate discouraging, as much as in them lay, of the slave traffic, both by making the engaging in it a higher penal offence, and by furnishing cruisers for the prevention of it; wisely calculating that while a serious River Plate war was staring them in the face, it was scarcely politic to be at daggers drawn with England. Slow steam-boats are often to be met with in this country, but I should scarcely think that steam had ever been so fruitlessly applied as it was to the boat, in which I took my passage southward from Rio, as with wind and tide in our favour, we reached the velocity of precisely five and a half miles per hour. Heavy brigs, more like washing tubs than ships, passed us deridingly, and men in row boats kept up an easy conversation with their departing friends on the quarter deck, with little strain to their arms or shoulders. In fact every thing seemed to be fallen into a state of repose. The captain, an elderly Portuguese, used to keep his berth all day, sheeting himself and snoring, and only making his appearance at meals, and then he yawned over his soup and his tea. The mate, to whom all management was consigned, used to take a sleepy observation about the middle of each day, but did not seem to profit much by it, as land generally appeared in a different direction to that denoted by him, and the pilot, a person of hazy appearance, was never to be seen except when actually wanted on entering or leaving ports. Our voyage to Rio Grande of some 700 miles, was therefore protracted to seven days and a half. For a bright smiling island, recommend me to Santa Katharina, it is considered the half-way house of the journey, and is situated about two or three miles from the main land of the Brasils. Desterro, the principal port of the island, rejoices in a good deal of traffic, it being a favourite provisioning and watering place for ships on their way round Cape Horn. Numbers of Californians put in there, in fact the little inn of the place was nearly full of American captains, who were just pausing on their way previous to the dangers and difficulties they were about to encounter, some of them in little schooners laden within two feet of the water, and yet none had fears of the result, all they wanted was to be off as soon as possible. There are some beautiful roads about the island, one I remember well on the sea shore, paved in some places by the rock over which the surf would come rolling in, washing the feet of the orange trees that poised their heavy delicacies over your head as you went along, while little distinct clumps of trees, round which the water had encroached and thrown up a barrier of sand and sea weed, would meet you here and there. The sea too was so fenced in by the mountain screens on every side, that no wind could reach it, and it came rolling its little breaking billows in so gently and peacefully, that vegetation never retired from its advances, but flourished and bloomed though quivering under its touch, and washed by its spray. On this coast shortly after I left, 900 slaves were landed from a ship, safe and sound, after two or three narrow escapes from the Rifleman, Sharpshooter, and Co. I met the captain, a very handsome and very smart Spaniard, who related his methods of escaping from the cruisers. He had been some few times taken and sent whither another great man had been sent before him, to St. Helena, where he had walked about and enjoyed himself in every way. He gave an excellent description of Longwood, and the other places which the mighty exile had rendered famous, and spoke very highly of our officers, who he told us used to shake him by the hand when they took him, and say "Ah, captain, is that you again? How have you been since we last saw you?" with an "Au revoir" at parting. He said he would be sorry to have our interference entirely removed from the slave traffic, as he could get much better prices for his slaves while it was carried on. To be sure he had to pack them much closer, and many more were wont to die than in the old time of slaving, and he used to have a cargo or two taken every now and then, but a cargo of 900 safe and sound at £50. a piece would pay for a good many casualties of that sort. It would seem impossible that there should be two places of such entirely opposite character in the Brazils as Rio Janeiro and Rio Grande. On one place every bounty of nature is lavished to make as perfect a country as there is perhaps in the world; in the other not one embellishment, no trees, rocks, mountains, or even patches of green can be discovered by the most persevering seeker after them. It would be difficult to find a place where sand had such an entire dominion; you are surrounded by it and sink into it wherever you go. To a casual observer it would seem strange how the 10,000 inhabitants who inhabit the eight parallel streets of which the town is composed, manage to exist, removed as they are from all the fruits of the earth in due season, no corn, no wine, no olives, no cabbages; sheep and beeves must be unknown to them, fishing must be their means of livelihood, and crabs or periwinkles their only fare. This idea, however, would result from a very casual observation of the capabilities and habits of Rio Grande and its people, for there are few places in the world that support so many butchers or where the inhabitants understand better the science of good living. The principal business of the place is the getting as much out of the "genus bos" as ingenuity and perseverance can effect. No Brahmin holds his sacred animal in such estimation as the Rio Grandensean would do, were he idolatrously disposed, and no besieged town after an excited soldiery have had the run of it, presents such a scene of carnage and blood as Rio Grande and its sister town Pelotas in the slaughtering season.

In the latter place especially does the red torrent flow; every tenth man you meet is a "Chourineur," and able to lasso anything from a mad bull to a sea-gull. The wharf at Rio Grande is covered with bits of oxen, hides, horns, hoofs, bones, and beef spread about confusedly, and the number of animals cut up yearly in the province amount to about 1,000,000. The feeding grounds occupy nearly the whole of the country, and the average price of a beast is about four dollars. Lassoing forms a prominent part of the education of the Campeiro. They begin as children with bits of string to lasso pins, from that they get on to cocks and hens, then to dogs and calves, and lastly arrive at the full maturity of the art, when one man, unassisted except by his horse, can go into the camps, single out the wildest and fiercest of the herd, pursue him, throw his lasso, and in a few minutes have him panting at his feet, helplessly bound and harmless. The men who are engaged in this trade, specimens of whom are constantly to be met with in Rio Grande and Porto Allegro, are as wild as the animals with whom they deal. A white wide-awake hat with many tassels, a many-coloured Poncha cloak, a yellow Charles II. sort of boot with its massive spur, a rugged beard, swarthy countenance, and dark eye, give them a highly romantic moss-trooper appearance; and in fact they differ but little from the William of Deloraines and Hard-riding Dicks of the olden time, for now that Rosas has brought border foray into fashion, the same feuds, the same mistakes about cattle, the same plundering expeditions, and the same border law are carried on at the frontiers of the province of Monte Video, as used to arouse the warders at Warkworth and Naworth and merry Carlisle in the days of Queen Bess. In the bay opposite Rio Grande, some relief to the general sand is to be found in an island composed entirely of mud, one of the most barren spots imaginable; there is one little house on it inhabited by some negroes, one of whom I surprised in my canoe when landing, and who straightway fled like a Man Friday. Innumerable crabs, however, make the place alive, and draw to it sea birds of every description, to get a closer view of which was the object of my visit.

Here the flamingo, the crane, the wild swan, the wild duck, and gulls of every description, are to be seen stalking, dabbling, and screeching, no one molests them, although within a mile of the town, and they pass their time amusing themselves and picking up a living without interfering one with another. The flamingoes are not quite the same as the great scarlet flamingo, being more of a pink colour in the wings and greyish in the body, but are nevertheless a most beautiful bird, they feed in bodies of twenty or thirty, and will let you approach within one hundred yards, when they begin to stalk very leisurely on, feeding in about six inches of water all the time. By making your approach as unperceptible as possible you can get very close to them, and then they rise very lazily out of the water and fly leisurely for some half-a-mile, the sun showing forth all the beauties of their coloured wings.

CHAPTER XVII.

"Water, water, every where."—COLERIDGE.

SOCIETY IN RIO GRANDE—BACCHANALIAN MEETINGS—PORTO ALLEGRO—BRAZILIAN MOSS-TROOPERS—A NATURALISED COCKNEY—A BALL ROOM—COCK-FIGHTS—A POOR MAN'S FUNERAL—A ROMAN CATHOLIC BAPTISM—BAY OF RIO JANEIRO BY MOONLIGHT—SUNDAY OBSERVANCE AMONG THE PORTUGUESE—THEIR ENGLISH COPYISTS—SERVICE ON BOARD A MAN-OF-WAR—DEGRADED STATE OF PORTUGAL—SETTING OFF TO THE ORGAO MOUNTAINS.

FROM the approximation to the Rio Plata country, the ladies of Rio Grande show many marks of Castilian origin, but in addition to the fair form and flashing eye, they inherit also the tendency to gallantry and intrigue, which has often distinguished the Donna of old Spain. It would be a perfect El Dorado for gentlemen of the long robe, and scandal would find her hundred tongues very much too few, were such things carried on in English society, but there Sir Benjamin Backbites and Mrs. Candours do not exist, and injured honour, impatient of writs and processes, quirks and quiddets, lies in ambush cloaked and stillettoed in dark corners of the street, and damages, if any, are always received by the defendant. I saw one gentleman (an Englishman by the bye) who boasted of scars in various parts of his body, received in this sort of way. With the exception of a dingy theatre and good duck-shooting, the amusements of the place are few, but fortunately most of the inhabitants have good ears for music, and many and pleasant are the little musterings of instruments and voices that take place at the houses of various merchants. This taste has, however, given rise to a strong under current of conviviality, and very often when the more classical and intellectual part of the entertainment is over, the English and Americans of the town band themselves together into little brandy and water brotherhoods, where the jovial and harmonious school of melody is much attended to. I was present at one of these "re-unions," when some sea captains came in, gentlemen of smiling features and limited ideas, three-quarters of whose annual existence is passed in brigs, of 250 tons, surrounded by hides and horns. It was a right merry sight to see these men of irregular appearance, with their eyes on the ceiling and their huge weather-beaten hands sentimentally extended, pealing forth in a Sou-Wester key the history of Poll and Sue of Wapping, or the feats of departed admirals and boatswains. After the entertainment, they rose up in their pumps (Captains of brigs invariably wear pumps and grey stockings on shore) and went careering down the street five abreast, trying to find their boat, but from the direction they took they were much more likely to find the Pampas first. A little government steamer, with a close cabin, carried us over the Lagoa dos Patos or Duck Lake, and two days stormy passage brought us to Porto Alegre. Porto Alegre or the Happy Harbour, is pleasantly situated at the mouth of the Jacuhy river, at its junction with the Lagoa dos Patos; the town is irregular and straggling, and the streets perhaps worse cared for than any you would find in a year's continental travelling, which is partly accounted for by the extreme scarcity of wheeled conveyances and partly by the absence of a Paving Commission. The stones lay wild and scattered, now opposing a flat even surface to the careful tread of the passer, now an edge calculated to pierce sole and body, and now a chasm, in which a month's rain had become green and curdled, and in which a duck might disport itself with infinite satisfaction. It is the principal frontier town of the cattle region, and the land mark of civilization; beyond it towards the west, stretches almost to the Pacific, the wild waving Campeiro, the roving grounds of wild-horned beasts, and the foray fields of still wilder men, to whom the sight of gore is familiar, whose trade is blood, and whether it flows from the veins of a panting bullock or fierce gaucho, whether human or [illegible]. I was fortunate in guarded by Brazilian soldiery, and the pencil of the often quoted Salvator would have found ample material in the group. One O Smith at a time is generally enough, but the vision of some fifty or sixty repetitions of that great Adelphi illustrator, walking the road of real life, was something too intensely unshaven and villainous to contemplate without wonder. Their arms and horses had been taken from them, and most of them were bending under the weight of their saddle housings and other horse trappings. Their many coloured ponchoes were hanging about them in shreds, their long yellow boots were cut and stained, and their sombreros and accompanying tassels were battened by weather and hard usage, over their rough, matted, bandaged heads; but from out of this villainous confusion, their dark eyes were gleaming proudly around them, like brilliants losing nothing of lustre from their wretched setting. Shico Pedro, the leader of the troop, of which these were a part, is a man of great influence on the Buenos Ayrean frontier, who had been waging for some time a desultory warfare on his own account with Rosas and his troops, provoked by the former aggressions of that successful chief. As this species of private settlement of wrongs was not quite in accordance with national treaties, the Brazilian government had been obliged to take notice of it, and these 50 or 60 men, foot in rest and petronel in hand, had been captured, to be kept in a political surveillance until war should have been declared in regular terms. I was the guest in Porto Allegro of an English gentleman, married to a Brazilian lady, speaking little but her own language, while none of a very numerous family understood their father's tongue. My host was a Londoner; but twenty-seven years in a foreign country had not in the least abated the strong cockney prejudices he brought with him. The Royal Exchange, the London Bridge, and the Regent-street of his boyhood were different places to those of the present day; but he said he could still take to Mark-lane, The Minories, and Aldgate Pump with all his old feelings. He was never tired of listening to stories of the old place, and the *Illustrated Lon-*

don Jose, which reached him generally ninety days after publication, was eagerly perused and intensely thumbed. Though my host was all potent down stairs, surrounded by his bales and his books, yet all the upper part was managed by his excellent wife in a manner that could not be improved on; for though wet paint on staircases to housekeepers had dominion over the rooms, though black babies swarmed in and out of every door-way, and though visitors were frequent, yet everything was comfortable in the extreme. The young ladies of the place were devoted to dancing, and would brave the dangers of the pavement and the night breezes for a quarter of an hour or more, in their progress to the ball-room of the town. Some ball-rooms and balls are very stupid affairs; and it must be the innate love of dancing that induces the owners of the twinkling feet to sit patiently out four or five hours, a silent muslined throng, arranged round a dreary room, waiting till the twenty minutes interval is over, and they are taken down from their shelves to enjoy a five minutes' whirl in a waltz, or a silent vis a vis in a contra-dance. After that is over, their cavaliers hurry away into an adjoining room, where they cluster round the ecarté tables, losing and winning their dollars till the girding up of the violincellos reminds them of their lighter duties. Besides my host, there were a few Englishmen in the town. In one street there are some half-dozen Scotch blacksmiths of very profane and dissipated habits. Being cunning workers in iron, they drive a very large business, but spend their substance in cock-fighting and general drinking. One Sunday, in particular, there was to be a grand celebration. Baxter's cole (as that worthy himself pronounced it) was going to fecht Jock Mc. Ginty's cole for a hundred milreas, and a great gathering was expected. I heard nothing more about it till Monday morning, when Mrs. Mc. Ginty came with two black eyes to complain to my host, who is always the arbiter on British matrimonial differences, stating that Mr. Mc. Ginty, having won the fight, had come home triumphant and ruthless, and that his wayward fancy had developed itself in attacks upon herself. Near the town is an excellent cemetery, laid out most elegantly. The niches in the walls are three deep and ornamented tastefully. As soon as one of them receives its tenant, it is bricked up, and the name carefully put on. As I passed out of the gate of the catacombs, two or three black sextons were lounging about, evidently expectant of something. In a few minutes a strange-looking covered vehicle, drawn by two mules, one of them ridden by a black postilion, booted up to his thigh, drove up to the group. Black-boots got off, produced a bottle of rum, and five minutes' revelry ensued. They then turned to business; the back part of the vehicle was opened, and a long coffin, covered with rusty spangles and tarnished velvet, was drawn out. The lid was opened, and the body of a middle-aged man, dressed in decent clothes, was exposed to view. This gave rise to much remark and display of humour on the part of the attendants: one dwelt on the texture of the dead man's coat, while another tweaked his nose, amidst the laughter of his associates. The death-bed of the poor man seemed to have been as uncared for as his burial; no loving hand of wife or sister had been there to press gently down his eyelids as soon as light and breath had departed; but his eyes, fixed and filmy, glared upwards upon the strange ministers, and nothing did they flinch from the grim and ghastly gaze. After a little, Boots having some other occupation in view, assisted his companions in putting the body unceremoniously on a litter, replaced the coffin, mounted his mule, and, bottle in hand, jogged on towards the city. Two sextons carried the litter carelessly to a distant part of the cemetery and laid it down besides a grave full of water. One of them descended with a bucket and baled out the water till he was tired, and then the dead man was swung in, the water splashing over him; the grave was hastily filled up, and the two men departed. A strange "good night to him" it was truly, but the last scene of all is not different to the general custom. After a body has been laid in state in a chapel, after the priests have knelt in gorgeous apparel, after the organ has pealed out its solemn requiem, and candlesticks have shed their

T

religious light over the funeral scene, relatives and friends take their last farewell; the body is handed over to rough careless hands, and instead of the simple but majestic "dust to dust, ashes to ashes," that thrills through the weeping circle in our own land, the last words uttered over the dead man in this country are those of ribaldry and scorn. Two days before I had seen a native baby of rich parents admitted into the Roman Catholic Church. The ceremony was being carried on in a small chapel to which I was attracted by peals of laughter, and found there the innocent cause of it all, surrounded by a merry crowd of friends and priests in array. The superior had the child in his arms, and his manner of tossing it up and down, poking his finger into its mouth, signing it with the sign of the cross, and sprinkling holy water, all which manipulations he performed confusedly, seemed to give immense amusement to all about him. The end, therefore, was only in keeping with the beginning. Owing to the terrible wet state of the interior of the country, further travel was almost impossible. The Campo was flooded in every direction, and a boat would have been almost as practicable a means of progression as a horse. I was greatly disappointed, for I had anxiously looked forward to the stantias or feeding grounds, and to catching a glimpse of the lassoing and the wild life of lassoers generally. But water coming when it was not wanted, and steam not coming when it was, kept me almost a prisoner, and it was more than a fortnight before I could resume my journey in any direction. At last I found my way back to Rio Janeiro, after endless delays, paying a visit to Santa Catherina the blessed. I entered the bay of all bays by moonlight, and when I gazed on the dark varied hills clustering around that quiet resting place, the lights of the town showing a brilliant fringe-work at their base, I almost felt as if I could have lain at anchor there for ever. We had to lie in rest all night, as Custom-laws did not allow of anything further than the captain and his mail-bags landing, and when the morning came I [illegible] to see that over the huge piece of nautical [illegible] which had loomed out uncertainly in the moonlight near us the night before, the English ensign was waving. On board, drums were beating, marines were mustering, epaulettes were glancing, and preparations were being made for something. A minute's thought suggested Sunday morning. It is melancholy to think how soon the reality of there being a Sunday morning fades away in a country like this. Weeks runs into weeks—the sacred landmark of the first day is passed over unheedingly. To the merchants it comes as a day of little relaxation; for, after two hours devotion to bell, book, and candle, in the chapel, he returns often to the labours of his counting-house, with the prospect of an extra time spent in the evening at lansquenet, with his select friends. To the trader or small shopkeeper it brings no relief. His store flaunts in its gayest colours and displays its brightest treasures till late in the afternoon. By the ladies it is hailed as a day of intrigue—as the day that brings round that delightful morning chapel where ogling and whispering abounds amongst the gay crowd that kneel about the painted shrines. By the public generally it is looked for as a day of fire-works and billiards. It is astonishing how soon Englishmen adapt themselves to the sad usages of the country. In Rio Grande and the southern provinces there perhaps was some excuse for omissions, for there was no approach to an English church of any sort; but in Rio Janeiro, where a neat stone building, cool and commodious, invited us every Sabbath, the congregations varied from twenty to thirty, and those complained of the length of the thirty-five-minutes sermon. Many of those who stayed away said they did not quite agree with Mr. Graham's (the clergyman) views on some doctrinal points, and therefore gave themselves up to shooting, billiards, and sundry other heterodox Sunday pursuits! To one, therefore, whom "bells had not knolled to church" for months, a service as performed on our man of war was something indiscribably grateful. Organs of treble power, music of deepest magnificence, white-robed choristers, "storied windows richly dight," in short all the tracery and panoply of our cathedrals could scarcely produce such an effect on a stranger as would the simple grandeur of the sea service, on a deck white as holystone can make it. Amongst cannon shrouded in colours, silent and attentive sit the chequered crowd. Clustering under the poop, in blue and gold, are the officers, from the pale-faced cadet on his first cruise, to the admiral, portly and pleasant looking. Forward, on benches, are the smoothed top knots of the well-scrubbed features of the sailors; while above, on the poop, glistening in scarlet and steel, are the marines, as stiff and orderly as discipline and pipe-clay can make them. Between the officers and sailors, the pulpit is reared, and thence, seven thousand miles away from home, surrounded by English faces and treading on English oak, one hears again the fine inviting language, and many-toned responses of our splendid Litany. It is a scene at once solemn and affecting, and every Sunday afforded a strange contrast to the service on board a Portuguese man of war, moored close by. On that morning, gaiety held her reign, and there the ship used to be perfectly surrounded by brats, which had borne to her crowds of smart ladies and cavaliers, who were engaged in dancing, fiddling, and riot. The thought would arise of what the country that owned her was now and what she had been;—of Portugal in the fifteenth century, and Portugal in the nineteenth;—of the splendid rivalry then carried on between her and her sister country Spain, in their efforts to colonise the new world, and to gain the sceptre of the seas;—and of their present degraded situation, their state the prey of needy intriguers, and their people the victims of the most degrading vices. The English side of the picture naturally follows, and the thought that our own country might have been in the same fallen state, had the holy influences of our Sabbath never been shed over her, and that had she bowed her knee to the same splendid Baals and devoted her Sundays to the same riot, she might, instead of filling her present exalted station amongst the nations of the earth, have been sunk as low and as irrevocably as her once proud rivals. I had much wished to take a journey into the interior of the country about Rio Janeiro, and had looked to the distant Orgao mountains as a blue boundary of promise, which I intended to surmount before leaving the country; and bearing in mind the invitation of my before-mentioned friend, the doctor, and looking forward to some of his pleasant stories and naval experiences, I made up my mind to be up and moving immediately. Had I gone according to the advice of some of my friends, I should have started bristling with dirks and pistols, but I applied to an old stager into the interior, one who knew every inch of the way, and who derided any such warlike display. He generally remarked—"You are a stranger; you have stabbed nobody's brother, nor intrigued with anybody's wife, in that distant region; and therefore need nothing of the sort." I took his advice, and girded unto my side an umbrella instead of a sword, and fearing nothing but rain and sun, departed with a stout heart, and on a stout mule.

CHAPTER XVIII.

"Over the hills and far away."—OLD CATCH.

SOLITUDE IN TRAVEL—MY MULE—SOMETHING LIKE A SHOWER—AN INNKEEPER'S REFLECTIONS—CLIMBING THE MOUNTAIN—NIGHT AT A BRAZILIAN MARQUIS'S—MULETEERS—THEIR "CHAFF" AND SALUTATIONS—A JEW INNKEEPER—WONDERFUL TRANSFORMATION OF A BRAZILIAN PONY INTO THE FLYING DUTCHMAN BY A PAIR OF SCISSARS—FIRST VIEW OF THE COFFEE PLANTATIONS—BED-ROOM FRIENDS—THE COFFEE PLANT—RIDES WITH THE DOCTOR—A COFFEE PLANTER "AT HOME"—"A MURDER OF THRILLING INTEREST."

THERE is a great charm in a companion in travel, especially if he suits your own inclination exactly, falls into your views, and is not given to disputation; but in some cases, I do not know, whether the pleasure is not even greater when you are by yourself, especially when that pleasure is found in the almost pathless woods, in the society where none intrude, and at the out set of a journey into an unknown country, with everything well ordered and pleasant about you. For it is then, that castle building, that pleasantest of amusements has its full swing, when fancy reigns supreme, and all the stories about young heroes, who have started on journies, well horsed, booted, and spurred, and after numberless reverses, have won their way to glory and matrimony at the end of the third volume, start up from every corner of the brain, each seeming to be an actual embodiment of oneself. The district about Rio is well villa-ed and ornamented;—in fact, it is only the total absence of chimnies to the houses, that makes it differ from our own Kensingtons and Bromptons. Four miles over this style of country brought me to St. Christovao, a distinct village, where the Emperor's palace is reared. Directly after leaving this, you turn your head to the mountains, along a soft sandy track, girt in by luxuriant natural hedges.

On the first day I only accomplished about twenty miles, not having started till late, and not wishing to tax too heavily the powers of my mule. He was a wonderfully sprightly animal, lent me by a friend, who never used him, but kept him in a yard with a cow, a pony, and a cassowary, where he did nothing but eat and enjoy himself; in fact it was difficult to hold him at first, so eager was he to be stirring. The next morning came dull and close, the mountains were not visible, the birds who had kept everything alive the day before, were now silent and drooping,—my mule's step had subsided into a settled workman-like plod, as if he knew something was coming, and did not think it worth while to waste any of his strength and spirits in unnecessary gambols. The way continued the same for the whole of the morning, sandy and flat, with a low green plantation stretching on each side, an occasional turn bringing a venda or shop in view, where travellers meet with every refreshment and encouragement for their journey. By and by, the rain came down not heavy for half-an-hour only, and then freshness and sunshine, but a continued straight down affair, against which clothing could do nothing, and I began even to suspect the impervious texture of an oil-skin saddle-bag, in which, not placing much reliance on the mountain laundresses, I had put many shirts the day before in purity and brightness. By one o'clock I had come to the foot of the mountain, and had arrived at an inn of uninviting appearance. However, in spite of copious assurances of hospitality, of alarming accounts of the dangers of the mountain when in a state of cloud, and of the immense distance to the next resting place, I thought it was better, as the mule was still willing, to push on. The road now totally lost its right to be called a road, for I have seen beds of torrents when summer heat has dried up everything, have a much more even and accessible appearance, than the way I had now to travel. The rain was coming tearing down, leaving in the chasms, mud of immense depth and stickiness. Progression was now accomplished by a series of plunges in, out, and over, the former most commonly. I had to do this too up a steep incline, in sodden jack-boots and great spurs, a large horse cloak thoroughly wet through hanging dankly over me, leading a mule, which had arrived at the greatest state of obstinacy I ever yet saw a mule arrive at, with the mountain mists completely shrouding the way thirty yards before me. But I had determined to do it, the people at the inn had said deridingly I would be obliged to come back, reconciling themselves to my obstinacy by muttering "Ingles," and I could never have returned after that, a spectacle of ignominy and defeat. Four hours brought me to a level, and the clouds began a little to clear away, but displayed exactly the same rugged features. A drenched negro in a little shed under a rock, told me that my resting place was still three leagues off, and it was darkening in, but our pace was improved, as I had sent the mule on before, following him up with an English hunting whip and the point of an umbrella, when he lagged, and by this means just came in time to see from a cleft in the mountain, the last beam of a watery sunshine, darting its dying rays into the windows of a large house, about two miles below me. The valley in which this house was situated was of great length, and a river of no contemptible width wound through the middle of it. This house seemed the only one in the neighbourhood, but it rose up amongst a perfect little village of sheds and barns, looking quite the residence of a lord of the soil. The mists had entirely gone from the low country, but the exact height of the mountains on the opposite side was undefined. I could see a red winding road up the side of the steepest of them, and I began to be apprehensive that the negro's three leagues involved the climbing of that. The rain had now ceased, the heavy incessant patter being succeeded by road-side waterfalls, which came bubbling out from every corner. On arriving at the bottom, two retainers of the owner of the house informed me that their master was a Marquis, and that the inn was some immense distance, in fact, I believe they made it further off than my former adviser. I therefore determined to seek hospitality of their master, of whose virtues they gave a most inviting account. I rode up and found persuasion little necessary, as I was most hospitably received, dried, bearded, and lodged. The Marquis, a man of very plain exterior, made himself very agreeable, for the little time I saw him, for early retiring and early rising is a distinguishing characteristic of the people, where there are no cards to keep them up till unholy hours. At first I only caught mere glimpses of the female part of the household, for Brazilian ladies, *en retraite*, do not love to be surprised by strangers, as they dote on dishabille, and wear more paper about their heads, and fewer stockings about their feet than they like any but their most intimate relations to be witnesses of. Two or three elderly ladies, grey and capless, and one young and rather interesting looking girl, joined us in the evening, during which the latter gave us a little music. The Marquis was very full of questions about England, and seemed a generally well informed man. I was up and off betimes the next morning, but found my mule's knee swollen and inflamed from a blow received the day before in his rocky leaps. A melancholy change had consequently come over us, our springy elastic step, our caracoling at starting had quite gone. However not wishing to shew our infirmities to our host, we put on our most gallant appearance till we were out of sight, and I then turned pedestrian once more. The mountain we were now climbing was higher than its opposite neighbour, which I had surmounted the day before, but the road was more winding, and less rugged; the morning was clear and bright, and the summit was unshrouded, the mists confining themselves to the ravines below, encircling the bases of gigantic trees, whose leafy tops brushed and wetted us as we passed along. The different ranchoes along the road were discharging their tenants, and strings of mules in single file, with their two bags of coffee each, came jogging down, all following with the utmost precision the footsteps of their leader, who, with his head adorned with flaunting ribbons, and musical bells stalked proudly and sagely in the van. In some places where the road was narrow, troops going in different directions would come in collision, and then the confusion was most ludicrous. The animals returning from the city had

V

no chance with their light miscellaneous burdens, in the concussion with the coffee-bearers. Their panniers would be torn down, and articles of every description intended for the delight and solace of Minas housekeepers would be exposed to view, and get terribly mangled in the mountain mud. This would give rise to a very wordy war between the black tropeiros of the the rival troops, and bad language would reach a fearful pitch, but luckily, it stopped there; for though most of them carried heavy sticks, yet I never saw one used in any of the many rencontres. The mules were mostly beautifully kept and shone resplendently: they were not so tall as the Spanish mule and the mule of the Southern States, but in point of symmetry were perfect. Their drivers were odd mixtures of mud and rags, and trudged away through the dirt and over the rocks as if their feet were of iron and not dingy flesh. Every one of them were extremely civil, and never passed without wishing you "Jesu Christo" and bowing most reverentially. This benediction they pronounce Zeus Croce, the meaning of which I was sadly at a loss to understand the first day. The top of the mountain was at last reached, but the view was much closed in from the interference of other heights, starting up from right under you. Still there was a splendid array of mountain tops, all covered with the richest foliage, and stretching out undulated and wavy, till they reached another range to the north-east, which reared its head, purple and majestic, above every thing around. A good sized town now came in sight, which presented such a capital appearance, and contained by report such a remarkably respectable inn, that I determined, to stay and see what fifteen hours' rest would do for my mule's knee, which had arrived by this time at three-times its usual size. The only drawback to the inn was its being kept by a Jew, who had a fine field for exercising the peculiarities of his race, and charged for meals and lodging about 50 per cent. more than the same accommodation could be procured for at the Euston-square or the Adelphi Hotels in England. He had a number of guests, but I had not more than three sleeping in the room with me, which was not many for the size of the room. He had a billiard table too, the only one in the place, around which all the unemployed of the town used to spend their days, and on which the marker and three or four guests of inferior note used to snore out the nights, their heads resting on the cushions and their dreams most likely of cannons. The deliberate opinion of a venerable hostler pronounced my mule unfit for progress in the morning, but he pledged himself to use all his veterinary skill, to make him ready for service in eight days, when I proposed returning and taking him back. I therefore had to hire a stiff ragged sort of a pony, as uncombed as a yearling, with a tail that dragged in the mud, and was whisked continually about him, bespattering himself and me in a most liberal manner. As this sort of thing began immediately after our starting in the morning, and promised to continue, I pulled up and docked him, giving him a racing tail, which much improved his appearance. After that we got on much better, but I was much surprised, that his owner did not fall into my ideas of improvement, for when on my return the pony trotted up to his stable, adorned with the first racing tail that had ever made its appearance in the town, that worthy was greatly astonished, and it was not till I had solemnly assured him that he was now "the exact picture of The Flying Dutchman, the finest horse in England," and that "the Queen of England had all her horses tails cut that way," that he was at all reconciled to it. Such was the general excitement in the town, that a large crowd followed me through the streets, and escorted the pony from the inn door to the stables. Shortly after leaving the town, the coffee plantations became very frequent, and some used to occupy the whole sides of hills of no despicable height. They present much the appearance of shrubberies of Portuguese laurel, allowed to grow to various heights, according to the age of the plant, and the manner of cultivation adopted by the owner. As I got on, the vegetation became more rich, in fact you seemed to be going through an endless shrubbery, so rich, garden like, and rare was the nature of the foliage. Parasites were just beginning to open out and shew their coloured glories, and birds in blue and scarlet became quite common, hopping and picking by the way side, as our little chatterers do at home. In one place I came on the body of a mule, which had sunk beneath his burden, and had been left where it fell. The wild dogs of the neighbourhood, were enjoying a rich repast off it, while around in an expectant but silent conclave, sat the oreboos or vultures of the country, waiting till their stronger brethren had done their meal, ready thereupon to commence their attentions which would not end, till the skeleton was left as clean and bare as any College of Surgeons could wish, to be blanched by the mountain wind. The second day brought me to the bank of a river, the boundary of the Minas province, on the side of which at some distance higher up, was the residence of my friend the doctor. I shall always remember the place I stayed at that night, as the very worst species of accommodation I ever encountered. The room was only partially roofed, and a capital view of the moon could be had by looking straight upwards. The bedroom was common alike to travellers and farm stock; a sow of immense appetite, a goose or two, and an infinite number of cocks and hens came in to see me at supper, and on awaking in the morning from a sleep, which though cloaked and booted, I had enjoyed most thoroughly, a highly disturbed grunt told me that the lady-mother of the stye had taken up her couch underneath me, and had no doubt passed a pleasant night. On first leaving home I had an Englishman's horror of sleeping in a room with a stranger, but twelve months had worked wonders, and here was I passing an unconscious night in a close approximation to a creature of more questionable habits than perhaps any other, and yet I slept well and soundly. A few hours ride along the banks of the river, during which I was asked to breakfast by a French blacksmith, who lived in a sort of jungle on the water's edge, brought me to my friend's house, who had not expected me to fulfil my promise, and was consequently much surprised. The coffee fazendas or estates, over which his medical care extended were very large, and the property of wealthy planters.

His house was situated at an easy distance from the dwellings of his patients, and he used to issue forth daily on a little long tailed mountain horse, of which animals he had a perfect little drove rambling about in his inclosure behind. I used generally to accompany him on his rounds, and wherever we went he seemed to be welcome, for as soon as the least glimpse of him was caught by any of the inhabitants of the negro houses belonging to the estates a yell worthy of the Sandwich Islands would be raised, and a whole swarm of black children would come rushing to meet him, and would escort him onwards with every demonstration of joy. A very fine building built of excellent stone, and the centre of a perfect district of sheds, sugar houses, barns, and every sort of convenience was the dwelling of the owner of the principal estate. He was enormously rich, owning 650 negroes who were employed and lived on the property, not merely for the purpose of coffee picking and preparing, but also for road making, building, and draining. His house was much too large for him, but he never rested from building, and an enormous scaffolding was then being erected for the purpose of putting up a new front to it. The decoration of the inside was of the simplest order, the thick stone walls and plain oak tables reminding one of the relics of the rooms of the feudal times. The first coffee picking was over, and the plants were in an intermediate state before the second picking came on. They were mostly about eight feet high, and in excellent order, promising well for the next gathering. The fruit grows in red berry clusters, each berry containing two beans, and has such a remarkably pleasant taste that one can not refrain from indulging in it on a hot day especially. Some trees yield an arroba, (32lbs.), but that is above the general average, and the number of trees there was about 60,000. When the berries are picked they are laid on a terreno, or drying ground, from which in due time they are collected and garnered up till the next troop of mules leaves for the interior. Our first visit to this man of acres and negroes surprised him at breakfast, of which he was partaking in company with a brother planter and his wife. The table was destitute of anything like ornament, and clad in the roughest homespun. With a beard of many days growth sat this lord of thousands feeding off the coarsest fare, and evidently enjoying it too. The lady had not had time to array herself in stockings, and was alternately feeding herself and a little ragged son, who coatless and dirty was seated on her knee. They did not mind about the doctor seeing them in this plight, but evidently disliked the presence of a stranger. Unbounded hospitality comprising black beans and farinha (the latter is the dryed mandioc root, but more like sawdust than anything) was instantly preferred, but we had breakfasted on something less savage, and declined. Dr. G. is looked upon as a great authority amongst these landed gentry, and whenever an alteration is to be made or a new project started by any of them he is always consulted. The district was generally an orderly one, the people leading sober discreet lives; and crime, unless in some cases where revenge is the prime mover, unfrequent. One rather notorious case though, in which robbery was the principal object, had made a great stir some little time before I was there. A planter, accompanied by a black servant, was returning from the city, where he had been disposing of the produce of his fazenda, his pockets stuffed with money, and himself in capital spirits from the good prices he had obtained. A few miles from his house he overtook a friend travelling the same way, and pressed him to be his companion and guest for the night. The friend consented, but insisted on the black servant being sent onward to inform the good lady of their approach. After some demur this was agreed upon, but the black servant was suspicious, and hinted his fears about this friend to his master. He however was sent forward, but instead of pursuing the road he jumped into the wood on the way side, and hidden by the underwood, kept invisibly journeying with the travellers. Presently he saw the friend drop behind, pull out his knife, and with one blow at the back of the neck lay his master a corpse. Having achieved this the murderer coolly rifled the body, transferring all the effects from his friend's pockets to his own boots, and hiding the body amongst the trees rode on to the house where the lady was waiting her lord's arrival. He was welcomed cordially, expressing great surprise at the non-arrival of the master of the house, who he said had left him to take a shorter cut after the servant had gone, and he was on the point of leaving to seek after his friend (so he said) when the black man arrived with the *posse comitatus* of the district, and charged him with the crime. The money was found in his boots, and the body was found in the wood. Notwithstanding these damning proofs the destiny of this bravo was not quite fixed when I was there, and I am told that there was some chance of his getting off, as the strong lance of justice is wavering, and often " hurtless breaks" in that wild country.

CHAPTER XIX.

"I do remember an apothecary."—*Romeo and Juliet.*

FOREST SPORTING—THE DOCTOR'S DINNER-CURE—A GANG OF NEWLY ARRIVED SLAVES—A BRITON'S RECEPTION—STEAMER FROM RIO JANEIRO—A SENATOR AND A PEDLAR—AN ENGINEERING SKETCH—BAHIA—CHURCH PAINTING—THE MINAS—THE BRIDEGROOM—PERNAMBUCO—BRASILIAN LADIES—MATRIMONIAL PROPOSAL—OLINDA—LIVERPOOL AGAIN.

AFTER a few days' varied amusement with my old friend, during which time we traversed a great deal of country, and saw every curiosity, animal, social, and physical, which it afforded, I began to think of returning. Our life had been somewhat on this wise. When our morning visits were over we used to ramble through the woods shooting at capivars (river hogs) or anything else worth powder and shot, but unless you penetrate very deep indeed into the forests, where you run a dreadful risk of being torn to pieces by "espinkas" or thorns, none of the higher class of game is to be arrived at. On our return, a rough but excellent dinner, flanked by some particular pint bottles of port, which my host always carried about with him, used to greet us; and this, assisted by some wonderful stories of the quarter deck and the cock pit, for the doctor was a perfect Captain Marryat when in the humour, made the evenings pass off most pleasantly. His friends, the lords of the various estates around, had been most attentive. On first hearing of my arrival, blacks heavily laden, one with a whole sheep, others with eggs, others with fruit, testified to the great esteem the "Dottor Inglez" was held in; in fact, my visiting him would have fortified his garrison against many an evil day, were such contingencies likely. To assist, therefore, in the general good fellowship that existed in the little household, some of the little parties that had travelled many weary miles for medical advice, would be asked in to dine, and really, considering their ailings, they always ate and drank most remarkable heartily. Ladies were often of the party, blooming mountain matrons, whom very often (owing to circumstances) it was more easy to assist off their mules than to hoist on again; as well as bashful young maidens, who kept their eyes steadfastly on their plates, dreading the bantering smile of their merry host, or the sly gaze of his friend. Their husbands, brothers, and lovers were often of the cavalcade, mostly well-behaved men, clad in the picturesque easy dress of their country, and I observed that they rejected black beans for English potatoes, and did not care about their accustomed Lisbon while the pint bottles were in circulation. After the advice and the dinner, which, I am sorry to say, is often "advice gratis, and dinner in," they would embrace us most cordially, and depart. It was a pity the last ceremony was not practised by the ladies. There certainly was one lady who seemed inclined to follow the example of her male relations, but she was at least fifty-seven, and from having taken too much of the doctor's wine, might have been pronounced a "pint" too elevated. Soon afterwards I turned my face homewards, and, by a different and more severe route, reached the town where I had left my mule. The hostler proved himself not a man of words only; for my animal, with his knee a little swollen, but otherwise sound and well, displayed all his old eagerness at starting, enhanced by having his head turned homewards, and probably by visions of his friend the cassowary and his old life of plenty and idleness. At about a day's journey from the city, in a forest gorge, which a lover of the beautiful might have chosen above all others as a lingering place, I met a gang of newly-arrived blacks, just set free from the horrors of a slave-hold. I could scarcely have thought it possible for such an amount of human misery to have been compressed into so small a number. At the head of the party, a devilish contrast, well ordered, well mounted, and well armed, was the conductor of the gang, a blunderbuss over his arm and

W

a cruel thong at his side. He saluted me courteously on meeting, but accustomed as I was to many forms of slavery, I could scarcely return his greeting; for struggling after him, bending under the weight of too heavy burdens, came the shambling crowd. It was a ghastly sight. It seemed as if the jaws of some mighty sepulchre had yawned, and given again to earth its wasted tenants, endowed with a feeble emanation of their old life. The glazed eye, as it was just raised in its suffering, and then heavily dropped, the white teeth that grinned from without their shrunken habitation, as you passed, told of another existence; and when you glanced at the figures—the bended, bone-pierced knee, the thigh that one hand might have clasped, and the ribs of terrible distinctness—the idea of the crowd belonging to the same order of humanity as ourselves, having the same hopes, appetites, and passions, instantly vanished. You looked upon them as such a throng of mariners as navigated the phantom bark to Heligo's Isle, or appalled the great Florentine on his entrance into Malebolge. The males had only a strip of calico round their middle, while the women had but a coarse petticoat hanging scant and loose about their shrunken forms. Their movement was very slow, but it seemed to suit their conductors both in front and rear, who, with their mules, were basking under the silken shade of their umbrellas most unconcernedly. The day was hot, and on passing a stream the party was allowed to drink, which they did, long and deep; but to see them, with their contorted and scarred forms, drooping over the water, bending themselves into every grisly shape, made one start, and ask oneself involuntarily, "Are these God's creatures? do these fearful shapes contain minds, and souls to be lost or saved?" The mountain breeze rustled through the wood, the boughs bent to its quivering touch, and seemed to utter the shuddering assent, "Aye; 'tis even so—'tis even so." No phase of British society is so pleasant as that which greets an Englishman travelling in a foreign land. He is looked on by his countrymen as a new slip from the old stock; as one who comes fresh from that place, which, with all the ideas and prejudices contracted in other climes, still holds the foremost place in their affections. The community may be large enough to be a community of sets, of visiting with this family and not visiting with that, but by them all the vagrant Briton is received with open arms, and if he incline his ear to the many little gossips that circulate about the tables of his entertainers, he may learn a great deal about the doings and the undoings, the virtues and the failings, of his countrymen; in fact, a good deal more of their natural history than they know themselves. But English hospitality, proverbial as it is, could not be surpassed by the attention and kindness I experienced from two or three of the native families of my acquaintance; from one especially in which I had spent most of my time, and of which I had been looked on almost as a settled member. It was therefore much with the feelings of a returning school-boy that I found myself again on a steamer, paddling for the last time out of the Bay of Rio Janeiro. I was facing homewards, certainly; but there was a rough Atlantic school of many weeks before homewards became home; and as the shroud of evening came darkly down, blotting gradually out many an object on which I had many times dwelt with delight, I felt it was blotting out with it, perhaps for ever, a transient home of much happiness, the vision of which, hallowed by the memory of three or four faces, clearly and constantly connected with it, will live in my recollection as long as memory holds her reign, as one of those bright associations of early days, which old age loves to dwell upon, and keeps garnered up in the store of fancy, though all be dark, seared, and cold beside. The steamboat voyage to the northern ports did not present many features different to what I had seen before; the boat was quite as slow, and the passengers quite as sick, but there was still plenty to amuse and interest. The occupants of the cabin were mostly senators and representatives, returning to their constituents after the labours of the sessions; and never were the *ouvriers* of St. Stephen's more eager to reach the murderous moors and partridge grounds, than these motley little statesmen were to scatter themselves over their *fazendas* and sugar estates, where they would hold imperial sway over their black subjects till the trumpet sounded again for action. They were the most indefatigable controversialists I ever saw. Although one and all were piteous victims of sea-motions, yet their arguments were not the less noisy, and though they often had to run away in the middle of a strong point, and contemplate the waves with concontorted visage for some minutes, yet they would return to finish out the discussion, without any diminution of energy and gesticulation. There was one senator who stood high amongst his country's orators, from whom these debates first emanated. He was a lazy man, generally keeping his little dog-kennel or deck-cabin all day, and his friends and admirers used to cluster around him, continually chattering and squabbling. My principal acquaintance was a German Jew of large proportions, pleasant heavy face, with massive gold rings in his ears, who had tried his fortune first in Europe, where he had been nearly starved; then in the United States, where he had been cheated; next in the West India Islands, where he had tried the American way of business and been ejected, and lastly in South America, where he was flourishing. He spoke with scorn of his own country, with appreciation of Jonathan, with disgust of the Islanders, and with pity of his present customers. He was very fond of displaying at supper glittering boxes lined with jewellery, before the eyes of his fellow-passengers, and very often to good purposes; in fact I have little doubt that he made his travelling expenses in that way, but to me they looked too German and lacquered to be attractive. Another great character on board was Mr. Daly, the engineer, a "Kings" man, (*i. e.* a King's-cross man) who had graduated in every species of low Cockney accomplishment, as taught in the neighbourhood of "White Condick" and the New-cut. He was a little man with a freckled impudent face such as London only produces, and was at once the bully and the wit of the whole "for'ard part" of the steamer. He used to sit upon the top of his cabin door, a position that no one who had not been accustomed to sit on the front rail of the gallery at the Eagle or Victoria could have kept securely, swinging himself to and fro ordering and "chaffing" everybody about him. He had a little fat slave into whom he had instilled a great portion of his own impudence, and whom he used to treat very kindly, and dress in his rejected moleskin. The little fellow would obey none but his own master, whom he looked on with immense respect. One of the sufferers from Mr. Daly's inventive genius, was the chief mate, a ponderous native, who used to be led a terrible life by his brother officer. The mate was ardently attached to pale ale, of which succulent he used to keep a little hoard in his cabin, and pull at when he was off watch. This was thought a fair ground for a practical joke by his rival, who having stealthily got at some of the best bottles, ingeniously perforated the bottoms of each with a small hole, abducted all the malt, filled it again with water, and cobbler-waxed the holes up again, leaving the corks and wires intact. The mate had no direct evidence as to the perpetrator of this assault on his pleasures, but the engineer was the only one who had the credit of the ingenuity, and he used to be hated accordingly. We reached Bahia or St. Salvador in five or six days. A few miles from land our bows were crossed by the H.B.M. steamer, "Sharpshooter," the terror of the coast, she was then engaged in the pursuit of a suspicious looking smack, which we saw her afterwards board, an act which made our Captain look rather uneasy, and he immediately sent down below half-a-dozen negroes, a little speculation of his own. For if the Argus-eyed blue coats on the steamer chose to consider that the number of blacks was more than our ship-books could account for, nothing would prevent their immediate bearing down upon us and examining. Bahia or the Bay is no doubt a beautifully situated place, but cannot be put in comparison with her sister city that we had just left. The bay itself is of immense extent, in fact in some places difficult to see across. The country about it is flat, indeed the light-house at the entrance was the first sign of land we saw. The town is situated on the bank, as you enter, a confused mass piled up on the side of a hill, that nearest the entrance being the ornamental end, and displaying much taste in villas and gardens. The wharves in the business part were lined with numbers of flat open boats, amongst which our arrival occasioned much stir, for as soon as our anchor felt the bottom we were surrounded and mobbed. The owner of one of them particularly recommended himself to me by his knowledge of English. On perceiving me he shouted, "Senor Misterre Inglishe, babbee boatee—I spik Inglishe"—"How tank you—berry well"—"I leave you my boy." This last Paul Bedfordism decided me, I immediately hired the linguist, and soon found myself at the wharf. A great deal of the locomotion in the town is performed in palanquins, which are very useful, as the ascent from the lower part of the town up to the higher regions is very steep and stony. To accomplish this, sundry pairs of sturdy blacks, bear between them a sort of covered pulpit, and run up in no time. The top of the hill and a very fine prospect are gained at the same time. The latter comprises a splendid view of sea on one side, and bay and country on the other. The principal features of the town itself are its numerous churches and monasteries, one part is devoted entirely to crypts and cloisters, with black-coated gentlemen droning in and out, in fact it is a perfect specimen of ecclesiastical ease in all its branches. In the churches more attention is paid to the rules of good taste than I have seen elsewhere, but some of the cloisters have the queerest specimens of painting. I saw round the walls of one a perfect old Testament history done in the blue pattern style, with much the same care of perspective and chiaro-scuro as those interesting plates display, and saints in all sorts of shapes and costumes are huddled together without order and rank. The blacks of Bahia are all of one race. The Minas, men of splendid mien, powerful, spirited, and stately-looking, men who if they could combine and turn upon their masters, might slaughter every white in the place, their numbers, four to one, giving them a resistless majority. It is strange though that no such casualty is feared, yet while walking about the streets and looking at the burly forms lying about lazily basket making, or bringing their knotted sinews into full play under some tremendous burthens, it was quite fearful to think how soon those forms and sinews might be active in another work, and how little would bring that work about. The Exchange of the town is a handsome looking building in the middle of cool looking trees, a feature in "Change" scenery as delightful as it is novel, in fact a little commercial bower, in which a merchant might almost forget that he was a merchant, and expatiate on the beauty of the country instead of the state of the funds, and play on Arcadian pipes instead of talking about sugar and cotton. From the little I saw of the English people, they seem a very united body of settlers, the "quarter" most of them affect is called Victoria Road, a pretty country way running along the top of the hill towards the mouth of the bay. Here the consuls of various nations live and bask under the colours of their separate countries, which are reared on tall poles on their separate grass-plots. Some of the villas, particularly those of retired slavers, are very tastefully built, and drooping trees of every form brush the passers by as they walk under the garden wall of each. While riding along a newly made road, I came upon a body of negro navvies, directed by a gentleman, who in spite of a certain climatic dress, looked so like an English country parson that I enquired of some friends and found such to be the case. The parochial charge and cure of souls being very light in Bahia, the clergyman has taken the roads under his care, and has added much by tact and perseverance to the progressive comforts of the inhabitants. The English community had just lost one of its fairest flowers, a young lady whom destiny in the shape of a husband, had claimed as its own, and was carrying ruthlessly away to Maranham. Among the many mourners for the loss, was a young gentleman with whom I stayed the night while in the town. He told me all the melancholy particulars, but as he seemed to have the materials of comfort, in three pairs of pretty eyes, the owners of which were awaiting *their* destiny at their father's gate, I did not think it any use consoling him. I particularly noted that gate, a green one with acacias hanging over it, and during my thirty hours stay in the place managed to pass it half-a-dozen times, but to no purpose, as the bright eyes were absent. The worst of travelling is that you get such a peep-show view of the many pretty things. That inflexible old showman, "Time," will pull another string before the little boys have got on their tip-toes to enjoy the first scene. The battle of Waterloo succeeds the view in Venice, before the delighted gazers have half seen the ladies and the lovers, the lutes and the gondoliers, and how soon, how very soon is the new scene passed and all forgotten! The Captain of our steamer had issued a mandate summoning all his passengers on board at five o'clock of the next day after landing. I obeyed and had the pleasure of finding that the bride and bridegroom were to be my fellow travellers. A little farewell festival had been prepared on Victoria road to bid them God speed in the steamer—flags waved, and little cannon roared from the houses of their acquaintance. As we passed out of the harbour, I could see handkerchiefs waving elegantly from the house with the green gates, but why should I remember them when none were waved for me? A crowded steamboat, where no stewardess is kept, must be about as severe a trial as a young honeymoon hero can meet with. My companion, however, was a bright example to all similarly situated people; in fact, I don't know what he didn't do, he seemed to be always running about carrying something, and when he and I did get settled to a quiet game at cribbage opposite his cabin door, (as sometimes was the case) a quiet sick voice would call out, "My dear," and there was no going on with the game till the voice was silenced; sometimes the voice would sound while I was reading alone in the cabin, and I had to run away to find "My dear," who was generally to be seen chatting with Mr. Daly, who used to laugh immoderately and wink at me most profanely whenever the message came. For the first two or three days the summons was answered immediately, but, afterwards, some little tardiness as shown, at which Mr. Daly would laugh and wink are immoderately than ever. Once, that little official, who was a derider of all good institutions, had induced him to smoke, and I heard the still small voice from the depths of the cabin gently upbraiding the naughty habit. We arrived in three days at Maceio, a little sugar port, where two or three ships were awaiting their cargoes. At this place a strange sort of natural break-water commences, called in the Brazilian language a Recêfe, which runs for eighty miles along the coast. Here, at its commencement, it was only a bar of sand, but at Pernambuco, where it ends, it is of solid rock, as trustworthy and as neatly piled up as any that Smeaton or Rennie could have desired. Pernambuco is the most easterly port of the Brazils, it was originally called the Recêfe from the breakwater, in order to distinguish it from the town of Olinda, about four miles distant, the original European place of settlement. The entrance to the harbour is puzzling, especially at low water, the time I saw it, for the reef stood out high and frowning, and the means of getting amongst the ships lying on the other side of it seemed dubious. After a few minutes' progress, however, a light-house at the end of the reef was rounded, and a placid lake-like harbour was laid open. The Atlantic waves without were beating in landward ferociously, now and then showing an angry wreath of foam over the top of the breakwater, but there was scarcely a ripple to disturb the many vessels moored within. Ships of divers sorts, and for divers uses, were here resting secure. There was the clumsy guard boat, the ever-watchful keeper of Brazilian harbours, ever mindful of its country and customs, but very regardless of its country's manners, at least as far as they are exemplified by its crew. There was the heavy Portuguese galliot with punchy sides and a Dutch bow, which had just taken as long to cross the Atlantic once as the Liverpool clippers had to cross twice and to take in cargo besides. There was the Brazilian schooner of war, a light elvish-looking craft, with a cut-water so sharp and sloping, and spars so raking and elegant, that you would think a strong gale could blow her out of the water, and that instead of keeping to her native

X

element, she would spread her canvass wings and flee away, despising the laws which bound her to her tempestuous cradle. There were the *jangardas*, the rude rafts of the country used for fishing or for the transport of sugar from the *ingenhos* scattered along the coast. These are built as much in defiance of naval rules, as the schooner in accordance with them. The deck, the pacing of which is always impracticable, is made merely of eight or ten logs fastened together. A straw hut reared on a little platform serves for a cabin; a paddle serves for a rudder; a large stone in a wooden framework for an anchor; a huge felucca sails supplies the means of locomotion; a huge bottle, hanging from the mast, the means of conviviality. Two negroes, who always completely represent the officers and crew, and adventurous travellers, fond of being uncomfortable (generally Englishman), represent the passengers. With all their odd elements these machines are very safe and fast, and can sail in any wind. This assemblage of craft, with the bustle of loading and unloading that was going on, and the constant clamour of busy negroes, made a very stirring scene when I landed. My first acquaintances in the town were made out riding, an evening amusement which every one who can, indulges in. The horses are very serviceable stiff-built creatures and are never shoed, which makes one wonder that their legs are not all knocked to pieces directly, judging from the furious way of riding that the Brazilian delights in over stones, gravel, sand, or whatever may come in his way. But even these wild equestrians could scarcely equal the Bedouin-like impetuosity displayed by one Mr. Midshipman of an H.B.M. in the anchorage, who was in the same riding party that I was. For an hour and a half did this mariner gallop his horse incessantly, till, as we were returning homewards, a cry for help reached us, and we found the little animal, which could not have weighed much more than his rider, lying on its back in a ditch, with two or three people trying to pull it out by its tail, and Mr. Midshipman standing by in a most forlorn state. The environs of the town are most attractive; numerous villas which, but for the absence of chimnies, would not look odd at Richmond, are situated on the banks of a bushy winding river, which coils itself twice into the heart of the city and is crossed by two bridges before it discharges itself into the sea. I was the guest of a native family in one of these villas, and saw a great deal of the people of the place. Sunday was their great festival, but after morning mess or chapel, which takes place at six a.m. the duties of the day were over. Company then arrives and Terpsichore reigns till dinner; then comes a long stroll about the river, parties of fifty or sixty walking with the regularity and precision of a boarding school. After this, dancing begins again and lasts till late. The notions of some of the ladies about English habits are very odd. One of their leading ideas was, that hornpipe dancing in all its branches was a prominent part of an English education, and they were much surprised at my two reasons for not gratifying them with a display of that "Surrey" accomplishment, firstly, because it was Sunday, and, secondly, because I had no idea of the step. Some of them amused me much by asking me how often Queen Victoria went to see pugilistic encounters, and if I was fond of cock-fighting. These two ideas have been gleaned from those dreadfully dissipated men, the engineers, who have established quite a taste for the latter accomplishment, one man coming out from Nottingham with a family of twenty or thirty game birds and a sprinkling of bantams, while the former scene is illustrated, frequently, with all the ropes, stakes, and rules, that are to be found at the meetings of Bendigo and "The Tipton," or any other Slasher. The Duke of Wellington was a person totally unknown to many, and Napoleon had just been heard of, through the medium of Georges Sand or Alexandre Dumas, but whether he was the Emperor of France or a South Sea Chief was a point they could not have readily answered. That every Englishman they meet rolls in gold as he travels along, is another error they fall into—an error which was amusingly illustrated by myself on the voyage from Rio Janeiro to Rio Grande. In the next cabin to the one I occupied, stretched out in the silent agony of sea sickness, were two females, a mother and daughter. They seemed totally unattended and uncared for. The first day I saw them I thought that the task of solacing and comforting them did not belong me, and therefore left it to the care of some brother, or husband, or friend, who I had no doubt was on board the ship. The second day, however, was passing without alteration to the sufferings of the invalids, when I saw on the table opposite a dish of oranges and a bottle of Bass's beer. Thinking these might be of service I brought them into the cabin and offered them to the sufferers. My offerings were accepted, and the relish with which the younger lady ate the oranges, was only equalled by the pleasure the elderly lady showed in drinking the beer. The next day one of the passengers, a civil, rather gentlemanly-looking person, came up to me, and after volunteering a general remark or two, asked me if I was an Englishman. On my answering "Yes," he said, "*Quer casar*," (do you want to marry). I told him it was a question I could not exactly answer without some deliberation. He then said, with a little hesitation, "I want to marry my sister to an Englishman, and as we are going to the same town I dare say we can come to some arrangement on the subject." I then learnt from him that the young invalid of the cabin was his sister, and that the beer and the oranges had made a deeper effect than I had imagined. On his pressing me again, I was obliged to invent the objection of "a wife and large family in England" as a slight obstacle to his wishes, and he went away apparently dissatisfied. I met the young lady afterwards at a ball, when I could speak the language better, but no reference was made to the negotiation. I found the Brazilian gentlemen well informed on many subjects, but seeing all their objects through a Gallic glass, by which their vision was slightly distorted. The town of Olinda, or rather what was the town, is now nothing more than an ecclesiastical ruin. It was the first settling place of the Portuguese, and was called Olinda the Beautiful, or, perhaps, Oh Beautiful, from the exclamation of the chief of the party, delighted to arrive at such a resting-place after the tossing he had experienced in his clumsy triremes. It is now nearly deserted; a college, the noisy young students of which were carousing in some mean *venda* when I went, being the only animated part of it. In fact, but for these sounds it might have been, a city of the dead. The moonlight, when I went, came palely down on shattered walls, deserted abbeys, grass grown streets, and shapeless stones, which masses of creeping green were fast hiding. There was altogether an air of ruined dark solemnity about the place, as the old churches cast their deep shadows around them, half shrouding in one place the white wall of a building as ruined as themselves, and, in another, rendering still more dismal the dark mysterious corners, where stones, skulls, and decaying images were heaped in woful ruin. One church alone, reared on the most eastern promontary, was at all exempt from the general decay. Time and tropical suns had laid a gentler hand on it than on the rest. The Atlantic was washing its base, and its shadow, deep and undulating, was thrown far out to sea over the calm silver ripples. An evening-song, the feeble effort of a faint organ and a few responsive priests, was being celebrated in it, but the sounds went seaward and tended little to relieve the general loneliness. The fishermen reposing lazily in their little white-sailed galleys, might just have caught the strain and "breathed a prayer or two," or crossed themselves at the sound, but no human being on land could have heard it, so stifled was it by the ruinous heaps around. The new town, formerly a little port and much despised by its cloistered neighbour, had quite cut the old. Its streets were bristling with energy and progress, while its founder, grown old and useless, was dank and deserted. Popular outbreaks have always been frequent in Pernambuco, and, in fact, if ever any republican tendencies are shown in the country, Pernambuco is certain to have founded and fostered them. The streets have often run blood, and walls tottering with cannon shot abound in the suburbs. The blood that flows, however, is purely native, foreign residents are comparatively free from harm, if they only keep out of harm's way; but going out to see the fun is as common there, where bayonets are the weapons and blood the result, as in London, where policemen are the assailants and little pickpockets the insurgents. I heard merchants talk of having frequently stumbled over the bodies of dead soldiers on their way to their counting-houses in the morning, and of stumbling over the bodies of fresh ones on their way back to their dwelling-houses in the evening, as a thing of no note whatever. By both my countrymen and by Brazilians my stay in the place had been made most pleasant, and on my departure to the ship which was to take me to Liverpool, a little array of the latter stood on the wharf to see me off, each of them embracing me most affectionately as I took my farewell;—my last farewell, with many regrets, of a people possessing eminently the good qualities that flow from the heart—warm affections, politeness without form, readiness to assist without intrusion, and the most unbounded hospitality. But England, that self-satisfied moralist England, will say all these qualities are more than counterbalanced by their vices, and will shrug her shoulders, raise her eyes to heaven, and thank Providence that she is not as other men are, and as long as every thing is to a certain extent *couleur de rose*, she can contemplate her children with perfect satisfaction and can cast a pitying eye upon the failings of all other nations of the earth, as if no Englishman had no vices to deplore, nothing at all to counterbalance our boasted blunt goodness of character. Rather let us thank Providence for a climate and especially a religion that has engendered a public opinion that scouts the degrading immoralities to be found in other less favoured countries. And if any weight is wanted for the Brazilian scale, let it be this, a thing to be carried as frontlets between the eyes—a Brazilian is never intoxicated. I have been in nearly all their large towns and in some of their villages, have seen them at home and abroad, where wine and liquors can be bought for an old song, and with the exception of an ignorant slave or two, and these most isolated cases, the only drunken people I have seen have been English or Americans. One of my friends, a sea captain, carried his civility so

Zeitfracht Medien GmbH
Ferdinand-Jühlke-Straße 7
99095 Erfurt, Deutschland
produktsicherheit@kolibri360.de